# WINTERSOL

# Wintersol

ERIC THACKER & ANTHONY EARNSHAW

Jonathan Cape
Thirty Bedford Square
London

FIRST PUBLISHED 1971
© 1971 BY ERIC THACKER AND ANTHONY EARNSHAW
JONATHAN CAPE LTD, 30 BEDFORD SQUARE, LONDON WC1

ISBN 0 224 00549 9

PRINTED AND BOUND IN GREAT BRITAIN BY
W. AND J. MACKAY AND CO. LTD, CHATHAM, KENT

To the meek
who will inherit the earth
only by forging the will

# PREFACE

THIS IS THE TALE of an enemy whom millions regard as a friend. It tells of the origins and early career of one who races like a spectre across our wintry skies, and descends from time to time to swivel a maleficent eye towards our camps and settlements.

The truth of this tale is painful, but nothing of that truth is left unsaid; though we must unsay much that hagiography and squalid commerce declare in regard to our protagonist.

Red cloak and snowy beard are talismans of merriment to many, but hereunder a tocsin is sounded in warning.

### HE WHOM YOUR HEARTS LOVE IS IN SOOTH THE ADVERSARY OF YOUR PEACE

Some truths can only be ignored with frightening results. Reality begins in confusion and ends in mystery; and, for chroniclers who, deserting comfort and shelter, have hewn passages through oneiric mountains and sailed the fifty-seven seas of the musroid* world, no illusions linger. We must tell our tale piece by piece, from the cataracts of its beginning to the clouds of its close, and the Reader must create his own refuge.

---

* Musroid: an adjective derived from the primal word *musrum* (Greek *mus*=secret + *rume*=force).

Life, between the confusion and the mystery, is a festival. Even the drowning mariner laughs at the dance of the waterspout. But, though the festivities of life have their own incredible logic, the Reader would do well to bear the following information in mind.

## THE MUSROID WORLD

The musroid world is a headstrong replica of the world we know, constructed on the principle that all conceivable and inconceivable things persist within reality, and that myth is the true history of this or any other world.

⁋ The inhabitants of the musroid world experience no life other than that of hazard.

⁋ Most of them were, at at least one time in their youth, shipwrecked.

⁋ The musroid world has been described by one authority as 'seedy'. This truism plumbs the pond, but ignores the ocean.

⁋ Musroid existence wears a mask of glamour to conceal its beauty.

⁋ Whenever the mask slips we witness the enchanting visage of Medusa.

⁋ The inhabitants fear that the Cosmocrator may cry 'Enough!', dismantle his construction, and seek some other place in which to reassemble it.

⁋ Musroid cities, dark and unrewarding, cower, dwarfed by half-completed obelisks.

⁋ Means of communication broke down long ago. At best, one nation eavesdrops upon its neighbour.

⁋ The musroid world is a vast, trampled battlefield.

⁋ Petty despots rule ephemeral kingdoms which subside at each daybreak from nightmare into daydream.

⁋ The staple industry of the musroid world is the manufacture of bloodstained bandages.

⁋ The history of the musroid world was written by gullible fools.

⁋ Is it possible to record the fortunes of secrecy?

⁋ Teratology must take the place of history.

⁋ The musroid world is a nightingale's sea-shanty.

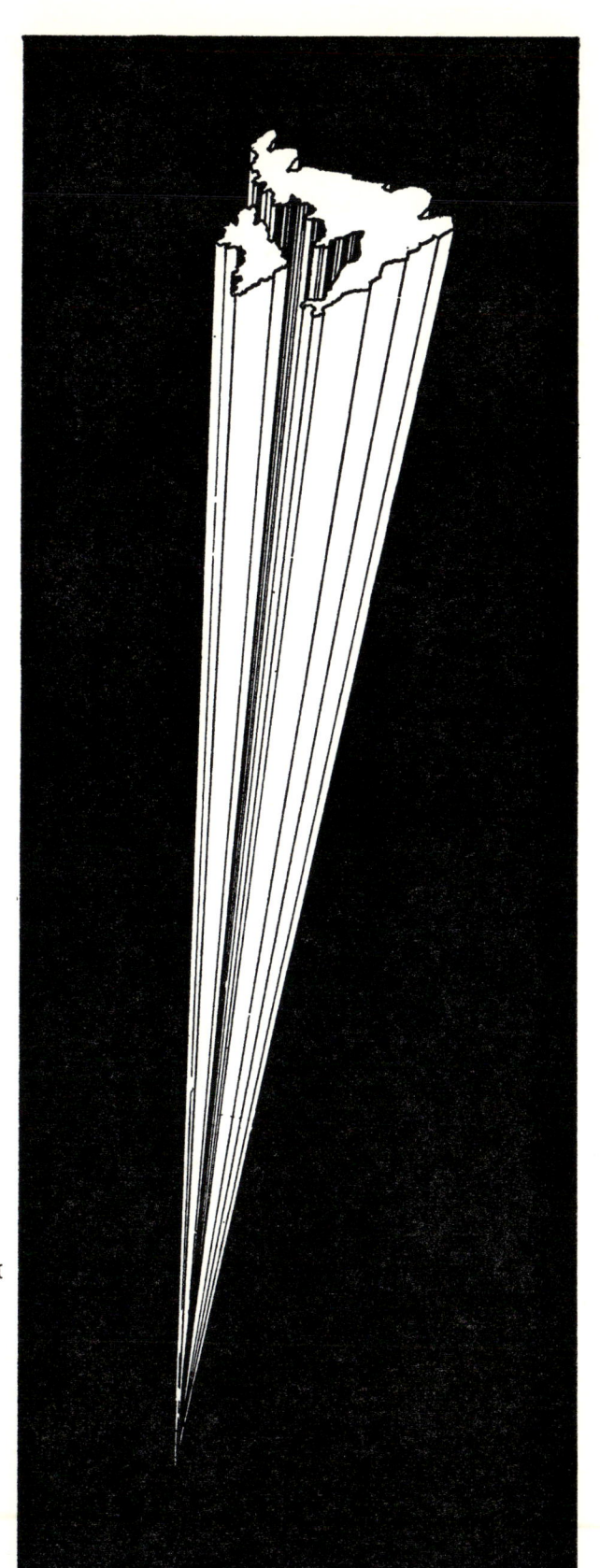

Fig. 1

# WEIGHTS AND MEASURES

It has been estimated that the gross weight of the musroid world is 6,057,000,000,000,000,000,000 tons. This prodigious figure can best be comprehended by analogy. A simple calculation will show that the weight of the United Kingdom, from its surface 'all the way down' to the centre of the world, some 4,000 miles (see Fig. 1), is in the region of 3,733,000,000,000,000,000 tons. It follows that if a titanic see-saw were to be built in space, the musroid world placed at one end, and a box containing 1,625 United Kingdoms at the other, equilibrium would be maintained (see Fig. 2).

As a matter of interest, this see-saw would need to be a large structure. Its plank would be some 38,000 miles in length and nearly 800 miles thick. The pivot would be a steel rod about 800 miles in diameter, and the two side-supports upon which the rod rests more than 4,000 miles wide.*

As a see-saw this cannot easily be matched.

* With acknowledgments to J. Holt Schooling, sometime Fellow of the Royal Statistical Society.

Fig. 2

# INTERSOL

Intersol is an island famed for its many iron mines.
¶ A long line of avaricious kings impoverished its vast mineral resources. The estates are now given over to the cultivation of weeds.
¶ The haunt of egret, unicorn and gazelle, it is much frequented by lovers of beauty.
¶ Hernando Cortes set sail from Intersol to conquer Spain.
¶ It was the only victory he ever regretted.
¶ Intersol is one hundred and forty miles square.
¶ Its weight is incalculable.
¶ In Intersol all coins and clock-faces are square. Balls are unknown.
¶ Intersol enshrines the nemesis of curves.
¶ If Intersol had never been invented, it would still be necessary for it to exist. It is the haven which we think we do not require.
¶ It stands as the last milestone on the road to the sea and oblivion.
¶ Eastward to Intersol: Land of the Buried Sun.

# GREENLAND

**C**ERTAIN PROPERTIES of the musroid world remained makeshift and ill-defined. They were restless, brooding areas, shunned by their bolder and more agile neighbours. One of these unemployable areas lay like a livid bruise on the brow of the North. From the safety of shipboard it appeared to be a blotched, unhealthy mishap.

The colours of the land led the eye on to roam, with ill-guided hesitation, amid siren promises of harmony. Whispers of green shouts of red and purple, moans of blue, grunts of brown, screams of yellow and white, squabbled in continuous, unresolved discord.

This careless appearance invoked the name by which this land is now known. Some unsung seafarer of the past, noticing the three most vociferous colours, daubed the place with the appellation 'Green, Purple, and Blue Land', but, in common parlance, this was soon abbreviated to 'Green-Land'.

Greenland was the most unnerving of countries, yet despite itself it provided asylum for a loose-knit rag-bag of malingerers and turn-coats. These tattered desperadoes knocked together a nameless settlement: a place even more lawless than its setting. The oldest inhabitants of the settlement were a notorious felon and his bloodthirsty consort. They were without doubt the most rascally among the tatterdemalion crew that infested the town.

# THE STOWAWAY

A LOST PIRATE BRIGANTINE roved the musroid sea. Whenever its crew ran up their ugly flag, twilight obscured the nearby shore. Ravens flew into the town to roost; moths, bats, and mice huddled in shadowy gutters.

❡ Listing helplessly, the ship cut its way through a stinking bilge-water sea, bearing a cargo of St Elmo's Fire, fireplaces, and fire-escapes.

❡ The pirates had long since forgotten home-port and sweethearts. It is doubtful whether the purpose and destination of their voyage had ever been known.

❡ Some among them claimed to be whalers; others believed themselves to be in quest of Eldorado.

❡ Inevitably, the brigantine came to grief in bleak arctic waters, the home of iceberg and ravening seal. All hands perished save one, a young stowaway. He escaped from the disaster along with the rats.

## BOOTY

One black and snowy night, this artful and faithless child stumbled upon the lawless town, and soon threatened the hard-won privacy of the ringleader's domestic hide-out. He proved an unwelcome intrusion in the town also, disrupting the querulous disorder even of that chaotic snakepit.

With typical acumen, he adopted the ringleader as his father. This unwilling guardian quickly came to resent a criminal dexterity even wilder than his own, and eventually cast the lad out into the slushy street. Not, however, before the light-fingered scapegrace had relieved the homely treasure-chest of four invaluable items. To wit:

>A Suitable Name
>A Diary of his Future Life
>The Portrait of a Beautiful Lady
>A Toy Factory with its Key

⁋ The name was curiously long and complicated, reflecting the devious imagination of its inventor.
⁋ The boy wilfully ignored it, and accepted with glee the nickname hurled at him by his frivolous playmates.
⁋ They called him CHRISTMAS, because he decorated their lives with dreams of excess.
⁋ This event he found already recorded on page ten of the Diary.
⁋ The Portrait was a trinity of wonders.
⁋ It was a plaything. Christmas saw in it the likeness of the most desirable doll in creation.
⁋ It was also a mirror, reflecting his brazen hopes.
⁋ Thirdly, it was a window. Through it he looked out upon the landscape of fulfilled desire.
⁋ The Toy Factory was his sole playground, which he industriously refused to share with his workmates.
⁋ It is the fate of all toys to be lost; and, sure enough, one day while Christmas was engaged in a furtive game of hide-and-seek, the Factory slipped unnoticed from his pocket.
⁋ He failed to find its hiding-place however diligently he sought.
⁋ A few tools and an oily rag remained as the only souvenirs of his lost toy.

## THE STREET

Christmas was dismayed. His darling Toy Factory was lost, his dreams were shattered, his heart was broken. But his boyish exuberance could not long be daunted. He resolved to build for himself another plaything, and so began his first rudimentary attempt at toy-making. The result was a Toy Street which stretched away endlessly in either direction. He spent his entire childhood playing with this toy. It provided him with every needful diversion, interest, and adventure. He tinkered with this compact world in zeal and eagerness. Travelling its undeviating length, he encountered ever-changing vistas of delight.

The Street was almost invariably deserted, but on rare occasions a bewildering flurry of activity sprang up. Processions, armies on the march, travelling circuses, solemn funerals, ambulances and stretcher-bearers, dog-fights, and other traffic passed by.

Sometimes the Street narrowed down to the width of an alley, criss-crossed by trip-wires, fallen trees, and other hazards. His nimble negotiation of these caused him to fall into the snare of self-congratulation.

In other places it became a slum. The houses on either side assumed a uniform appearance of age, squalor, and dilapidation. Ill-kept children squabbled endlessly as they played their mean games in the filthy gutter. Slatternly women shrieked abuse at the luckless lad; drunkards sprawled in doorways; footpads filched his pocket-money; blind beggars shuffled by; bawds flaunted their dubious charms without shame; violent accidents occurred all the time.

His bruised spirits healed rapidly as the Street once more became a broad thoroughfare. Brightly illuminated shops abounded, vying with one another for his custom as they boldly displayed their merchandise.

A glamorous toyshop captured his attention. Regrettably, the prices asked for its marvellous wares confounded his meagre pocket. This deprivation stimulated an untrammelled, passionate craving for all the good toys in life.

The shops gave way to rich dwellings on either side. Christmas peeked through intimate windows to observe coquettish ladies and courteous gentlemen engaged in elegant sport. Wine and music were flowing. Revellers, both noisy and silent, were celebrating some mysterious triumph. He was mystified by these goings-on, and dark, unnameable fears flickered in his breast.

## SCHOOLS

Christmas's education began immediately after his tenth birthday. It occurred to him that certain of the Street's buildings invited exploration; and as a result of this pursuit he discovered the sources of his vast future erudition. Amid the hodge-podge of the Street, he came upon numerous thinly disguised academies. He enrolled as a student forthwith, and in due course of time, the whole Street became for him a classroom. Everything in it was grist to the mill of knowledge. The world was his blackboard.

# PLAYTIME

Christmas was, above all, studiously interested in toys. Delighted by the signal success of his first essay in toymaking, he resolved to do special research into the origins and natural history of these endearing trivia.

Unfortunately, most of the boy's attempts at toymaking were fiascos. Failed toys lay abandoned in the Street: a profitless clutter of stillborn delights. Freak runaway playthings careered out of control along the Street, and were the cause of spectacular crashes in which great numbers of innocent spectators were damaged.

But not all his endeavours were abortive. Some of his products ran as smoothly as oiled clockwork. They were wilful and sinister, and those into whose hands they fell became, willy-nilly, the playthings of the toys.

Many of his toys were dangerous. They became even more so when broken.

So, in addition to being a classroom, the Street became a playground. This led Christmas to take an interest for the first time in the other inhabitants of the Street. He realized that he needed them to help him to control his accumulating hoard. Furthermore, he knew that they were merely accessory parts of his original toy, things to be used for his own pleasure and purposes. Their only reason for existence was to be his servile playmates.

Recruitment had sometimes to be facilitated by bribes. He was ever wary of parting with any of his precious toys, but he had other, less tangible gifts to bestow.

These dealings occupied the hours of both the day and the night. The daytime he devoted to the men. With them his bartering was open and unashamed. At night the more stealthy aspect of his trade asserted itself as he stole into the homes of women to bestow his nocturnal favours.

Christmas was more terrible than any burglar.

With the endearing image of the lovely lady's Portrait always hanging in the gallery of his mind, he scornfully criticized the cheap copies which necessity compelled him to handle.

# LOCKED-OUT

During one such midnight excursion Christmas blundered into a stretch of the Street hitherto untouched by his boot-shod feet. It was an abandoned industrial area, in which various workaday structures and enclosures sat idly side by side. Each was boarded up and devoid of life. Begrimed signs hung askew from every gate:

> NO
> HANDS
> WANTED

Dead-end alleys led off from the Street, and the susceptible child was quite unable to resist the invitation of their beckoning emptiness. Venturing into one such alley he espied, framed in a jagged hole in the bleak, blank wall, a nostalgic yet menacing vision. Across an intervening expanse of wasteland loomed the outline of a hauntingly familiar edifice. His heart somersaulted within his breast. He knew that building! It was his long-lost Toy Factory. He clambered joyfully through the jagged frame, and sprang to recover his pilfered prize.

As he sped across the desolate land he deftly studied its more noteworthy aspects. Other than the scavenging birds and omnivorous vermin, the only sign of life was the Factory — a grimy industrial conglomeration, ever astir. Uttering its predatory din, it raided the scrapyards, slaghills, and shallow quarries for raw materials and fuel. By dint of a superlative spurt, he arrived at the Factory gate, only to find himself locked out like any tardy workman. The gate was barred and padlocked, and no matter how hard he worked, banging and hammering on the featureless metal, he could not refashion the fact of his exclusion.

A swift circumambulation enabled him to observe, with increasing resentment, the varied components of the Factory complex. He glimpsed, beyond the wire fences and wooden palings, a dizzying confusion of activity.

As an outcome of his studies, Christmas confirmed his earliest impression that this was no commonplace factory. By some blind knack of self-genesis it was visibly creeping like a malignant lichen across the landscape. Additional sheds and workshops formed like cells around its perimeter. Foul dross and noxious slag oozed from its wastepipes; molten pig-iron swilled forth on to the squealing earth. From its many vents and ducts issued uncontrolled jets of steam, sticky black lubricants, and garish powders, pink, blue, and green, which besmirched the shrivelled face of the land.

Christmas was young, and springtime troubled his blood. He fell even more hopelessly in love with the Factory, and planned amorous conquest. He retraced his rapid steps towards the spot where he had left the Street, intending to marshal his well-schooled and docile playfellows. Consternation greeted him with mocking salute. Having rediscovered one plaything, he had inadvertently mislaid another . . .

The Street had disappeared.

## THE ROOM

With heavy feet and heavier heart he trudged Westward, mocked by the hoots and whistles of the distant Factory. A dark congregation of birds speckled the lowering sky ahead. His listless feet quickened as he speculated upon the reason for this urgent gathering of gulls and crows. He raced into the midst of the ravening birds, flapping his arms like a wind-torn scarecrow, and the affrighted birds dispered, cawing and whining. There before him was the sole souvenir of the vanished Street.

Out of all the multifarious rooms and apartments which Christmas had once known and explored, only one example remained. Without pausing to ask why this alone had been left, he pushed open the Room's rickety door and passed out of the chilling rain.

In a mood of interwoven acceptance and hope, he crossed the threshold to begin his occupancy. It was to be the last room he ever lived in during his long and alarming life.

## AN INVENTORY OF THE ROOM'S EFFECTS

*Item:* a sickly carpet fed upon by herds of grubs and schools of silverfish.
*Item:* a table which never needs dusting.
*Item:* a chair which needs dusting all the time.
*Item:* a deathbed.
*Item:* a complete set of broken crockery.
*Item:* twenty silver knives decorated with thieves' fingerprints.
*Item:* eighteen forks bearing the odour of old mouths.
*Item:* a stuffed spoonbill.
*Item:* a large cupboard with one half-open door, containing jars of live-bait and several panes of coloured glass.
*Item:* a handwritten inventory of the items listed above.

## CHRISTMAS AT HOME

Celebrating the arrival of a fresh contentment, Christmas bestowed several uneaten meals upon importunate Eskimos. Then, in a glow of satisfaction, he stood pensively beside his table and drew from his haversack the remaining items of his loot. He laid the Diary, with its faithful pen, upon the table, and reverently suspended the lady's Portrait from a copper nail in the Southern wall. The Diary offered its secrets, silent as falling snow, to his inquisitive eye; the lady's image smiled down upon his Northern enterprises – the Helen of his stirring dreams.

Only when all this was achieved did Christmas consider that he had a home adequate to his immediate purposes.

During the year of his tenancy he proved the truth of the old saying that 'one does not have to be seen in order to exist.' He also perfected several recherché techniques of escape. The latter were to serve him well during the adventure which shaped him into the rapscallion all now know him to be.

To idle away his time, Christmas perused twenty pages of his Diary. His pride of acquisition grew steadily as he read.

# BELLA: HER CUNNING WILES

BELLA, the most beautiful woman in the musroid world, was born in Rome during the freak winter of 1881.
⁋ Seagulls and curlews echoed her birthcry.
⁋ After a cursory babyhood she achieved the age of slippery guile.
⁋ To celebrate this event, she wrote a palinode in which innocence was castigated.
⁋ Her hands were whiter than unfiltered light.
⁋ In a city where deceit was deemed a virtue, she fell in love with a life of respectable crime.
⁋ Bella inherited two silver wheels. By means of these she travelled far and wide.
⁋ Men feared her. Women hated her. Children endured her. Foxes outwitted her. Falcons stooped to her. Only the blind walls ignored her.
⁋ By the time she was eight years old she was so radiantly lovely that most of the sunsets and rainbows migrated in search of their lost admiration.
⁋ Bella is a paragon of scandal.


# BELLA: HER WINNING WAYS

⁋ Bella shone her lamp into the eyes of the blind.
⁋ Her chameleonskin gown always assumed the colour of her own flesh.

⁋ She built a city in the shape of a tree.
⁋ When the citizenry rebelled against her she chopped the city down.
⁋ In a former existence Bella was a silver wheel.
⁋ The wheel left a rut which filled with clear water, the haunt of darting fish.
⁋ Bella's twin sister was a kingfisher: a denizen of the banks of the rut.
⁋ Bella owned a copper coin with which she purchased all her worldly needs.
⁋ She slipped a ring from her finger and gave it to the poor.
⁋ Thereby poverty was banished from the world.
⁋ Bella built a village in the form of a flower.
⁋ When the villagers murmured against her she plucked the village for her hair.
⁋ Bella is the world's nosegay.

## BELLA: HER COSMETICS

⁋ Bella was the embodiment of wonder. She dedicated her beauty to Outrage, her vivacity to Licence.
⁋ For her thronging legion of moods she distilled a wide array of cosmetic preparations. They embraced the colours of Mystery, the odours of Calumny, the textures of Adoration.
⁋ Her rouge mocked the blush of shame.
⁋ Her powders were disguise for an innocent malefactor.
⁋ Her lip-paint glowed like revenge.
⁋ Her lacquers and varnishes had the sheen of pride.
⁋ Her perfumes were nameless anaesthetics.
⁋ After anointing her body with fragrant creams, she would wipe them off on her lover-of-the-day.
⁋ Bella's handmaidens burnished her fingernails to mirror-brilliance, and thus she bemused the minds of her more narcissistic lovers.
⁋ Her perfumed camouflage kept her inviolate in the manoeuvres of each *affaire*.
⁋ Bella is a gilded nightshade.

# BELLA:
## HER UNWILLING EXILE

⁋ Beyond the litter-yards, beyond the hoardings, beyond the ditches and weeds, towered Bella, immaculate and rare ... our whitest *lusus naturae*.

⁋ Her lovers included a blindfolded prisoner and his firing squad, the sentry of the kitchen garden, and a blackbird trainer.

⁋ Her scrivener secretly addressed all her love-letters to himself.

⁋ Bella wore a red wig in memory of Garibaldi.

⁋ She dreamed of Garibaldi day and night.

⁋ Bella came to Intersol in 1896, believing it to be Garibaldi's last stronghold.

⁋ Touring Intersol in the company of wolves, Bella discovered the glacial Northern coast, previously unknown.

⁋ She was haunted by the snowstorms that raged at her nativity. Still they taunted her. Still they eluded her. In a fury of desire, she hunted them throughout the Northern Province.

⁋ In the warmth of her presence the glaciers melted away.

⁋ In the icicled grotto of her mind ill-clad dreams huddled together for comfort.

⁋ In Northern Intersol she built her December Palace, and waited hopelessly for a winter that never came.

⁋ Bella is a fish out of water.

## NURSERY DAYS

The favourite idol and diversion of Bella's girlhood was a working scale-model of a Northern town. It was the most exciting among the many acquisitions of her tenth birthday. It had no name, but she recognized it nevertheless, cooing over its elaborations. As her guardians either hoped or feared, it revealed to her the delightful menace of an outside world.

How sweet it is to be ten, when one has only been nine before!

Throughout that sombre birthday, while ravenous cattle gobbled fodder in their shed, Bella's imagination grazed over this strange construction. The snow glittered on every rooftop. Sleigh-ruts patterned the slush of every street. Winds moaned round the eaves and whipped her pale hair against her cheek.

Cabins, saloons, and stores, perfect in every minute detail, studded the centre of the board. At the edges, desolation reigned. The views to the South, East, and West were identical with the view to the North. In the latter direction nothing could be seen at all. Bella ignored those moaning wastes and let her eye wander inquisitively through alley, court, and cubbyhole. The inhabitants of the town, occupied for the most part by male venality and female cajolery, were oblivious of the dainty explorer.

Stung by their indifference, Bella yearned for diminution. If only she could become a working scale-model of herself, she would enter with zest into the noiseless violence of the streets – the knifings, the lootings, the popular revolutions, the entire black gaiety of this Northern microcosm. Obviously her wish could not be granted, yet, in her rabid imagination, she played out many a convincing game.

She sided with the Urchins against the Ragamuffins in the Great Snowball War. She participated in the Sack of the Patrician Heights. She lured the Sleepy Emperor from the joys of his Illicit Harem.

Only after many breathless hours of unhallowed amusement did the girl awaken, and then with a weird shock of deprivation. She became aware that her new toy was incomplete. Two parts were missing. Hard by the town centre a lettered site advised:

AFFIX FACTORY,<br>
ROOM, OR<br>
STREET HEREON

In the sunny Southern outskirts another void space invited:
>AFFIX STREET,
>ROOM, OR
>FACTORY HEREON

Chagrin swept Bella. The discovery of these omissions shattered her delight, and restlessness would rule until those missing parts were found and the toy's pristine state restored.

# SEARCH AND DISCOVERY

A solitary figurine caught her bloodshot eye. One of the Ragamuffins had quit his gang, and stood now, legs apart, arms akimbo, beside the second empty site. Incensed by the committed arrogance of the young Turk's expression, Bella snatched him up and hurled him furiously against the nursery wall. A spectacular ricochet landed him amid a heap of soiled doll-dresses and undergarments in a forgotten corner.

The corner remained forgotten. Bella's vexation simmered for a full week before modulating to fretful melancholia. Then, tugging this dun blanket of sorrow round her, she began a half-hearted search for the missing parts. Right, left, east, west, south, north, upstairs and downstairs she sought. In her favourite nook, in her secret cranny, in the gardens and beyond, down the path and over the bridge to the trees and the coast. Atop the highest dune, she peered out over windswept links and sunswept waves. Of her quarry she saw no sign.

Back in the nursery she ransacked her toychests in vain. But, suddenly, the rubicund visage of the outcast mannikin peered into her distraught memory, impudent as ever. Strangely stirred, she rummaged idly among the stained dolls' garments. Somewhere here the lout was hiding. She found him without undue difficulty and threw him back into the town. So much for him! But something

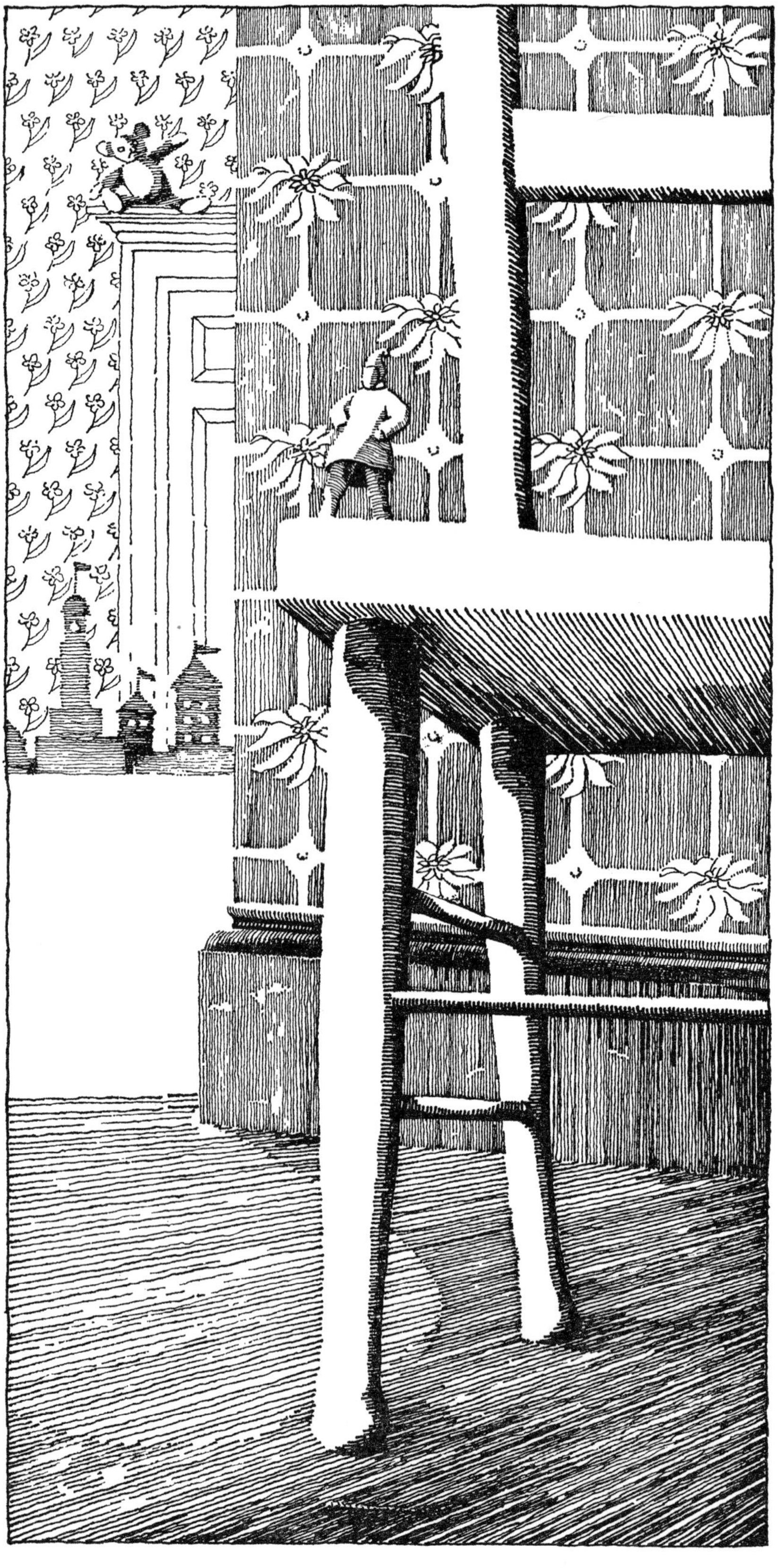

whispered to Bella that a further discovery might ensue. She killed time by sorting the garments, and soon her hand encountered an enigmatic shape veiled by the soft fabrics. Slender fingertips extricated the object; pink lips parted in a squeal of joy. It was not a room, neither was it a street. Only one possibility remained.

With fluttering heart she skipped back to the town and lowered her new-found treasure into the central site. It fitted into place with a gratifying click, and within seconds black plumes of smoke billowed from its many chimneys.

What is a town without a factory?

# A LUCKY DIP

STRANGE FEATURE OF REALITY is the tendency of certain beloved objects to surround themselves with an aura of prohibition. Bella's oldest plaything – her bran-tub – had, for some time, denied her the outré satisfaction of the many lucky dips which had once enriched life with gewgaws both humorous and perilous. Her arm ached for the warmth of the yielding bran.

One day, however, a girlish intuition prompted her to approach her estranged friend with renewed confidence. A first investigation suggested that the bran was mockingly empty of packages; but then her desperate fingers gained purchase on an object of tantalizing form. Drawing it forth, she dusted it, and carried it Southward tremblingly.

The slender package took an age to unwrap, but Bella did not outstrip her girlish excitement. She recognized at length that her darling tub had rectified the second omission. The Street, for such it was, proved tailormade for the Southern site. And what an absorbing acquisition it was, more absorbing by far than the rest of the town. It inspired her to act out her fantasies of diminution with even bolder extravagance. It became her thoroughfare of dreams, and her fancy lost itself so completely here that other districts of the town remained disastrously ignored.

Returning to herself one evening, Bella encountered the woeful outcome of her folly. The Factory, so recently retrieved, was gone from its central site. Too weary to search, she was compelled to leave the matter until morning and, by then, renewed zeal for the Street blotted out everything. It was evening again before she thought of the Factory.

And so, we must dismally record, it went on ... infatuation at dawn; desolation at dusk ... and, inevitably, the Factory became more lost than ever. Futile for the pallid nymph to advise herself that the Street held alternative factories galore. It must have been obvious, even to the most work-shy, that all these had been closed for years.

She mooned through adolescence with an impaired scale of judgments, revelling in the illicit lures of the Street, while acknowledging in more sober hours that her little model world was unbalanced and awry. She was driven to invent more desperate modes of amusement, and the nursery walls threw back her hollow laughter, day after day.

Small wonder that she welcomed the onset of womanhood, and the discovery of more sophisticated games, with a certain relief.

## BRIDGES

⁋ Perceiving the need for a link between herself and one of her lovers, Bella cultivated two sweet-smelling gardens that arched and intertwined across a prohibiting valley.
⁋ Bella constructed a bridge that gave access from her chambers to the next town.
⁋ The wolves had a bridge that rode over the heads of their foes to their prey.
⁋ Bella ordered her engineers to build a bridge to connect Intersol with Malta. With half the task accomplished, she changed her mind. The structure was then converted into a castle.
⁋ Bella owned more bridges and more rivers than any other lady in the musroid world.
⁋ She instructed her handmaidens to stitch a silken bridge to join her golden gown to her silver cape.
⁋ She caused stepping-stones to be erected across a streetful of swift traffic.
⁋ Bella is a silver bridge astride a milky river.

## A PRISONER OF THE SOUTH

The year of keenest loneliness was 1899. Bella dismissed her duenna, the last of her human companions, and retired to the innermost chamber. There she embraced the cult of invisibility, and soon

*Bella's Dream*

became so slyly camouflaged that even her favourite mirrors failed to recognize her. In time she wearied of this puerile hobby and sought to recapture the festival of youth. But her nostalgias reaped no restoration. Life was a broken whirligig. Even the graveyard failed to cheer her.

Remorseless summer prevailed in Intersol. Munificent sunlight tormented the day. Even the moonlight was warm. And Bella, dreaming of the sharp kiss of snowflakes, the jag-toothed smile of icicles, fanned her exhausted flesh in the penurious shade.

Why did fortune ignore her requests? Garibaldi would have given her the snows. Encased in his scarlet shirt, he would have scoured the ice-floes of the world, he would have traversed the very Poles to bring her arctic entertainment. Thank heaven, her vision of Garibaldi survived scatheless to console her in the oven of her sorrow.

To Bella, Southerner though she was, the South seemed extravagant, wasteful, pampered, and inebriate. She had never gazed upon the snowy hummocks of the North, but she knew that those wintry wastes were her true habitat. Albeit, her pathetic attempts at winter counterfeit were desperate gestures, mere shadowplay. Proud summer held this pretty malcontent in thrall.

Her wolves remained faithful, but, sad to say, a melancholy change had overhauled these feral companions. Their claws atrophied, their fangs lost their needle sharpness, their coats mislaid their sable sheen, their howls modulated to lapdog ululations. Looped with pearls, restrained by jewelled collars and silken leashes, they sniffed the sybaritic perfumes of truce.

In desperation Bella ransacked the treasury and brought forth the trivia of her snowbound girlhood. Soon the contents of her chests cluttered the Palace from end to end. Dolls nodded to her admonitions; clockwork trains arrived and departed at her signal; golliwogs muttered tribal conundrums; teddy-bears terrorized the wolf-packs; balls bounced; shuttlecocks flew; jacks sprang from boxes; penny-whistles screamed . . . But the enchantment of this outrageous toyland quickly soured.

# GOLLIWOGS: EXTRACTS FROM AN OLD NURSERY MANUAL

OLLIWOGS are models of our darkest thoughts, fell homunculi devised by an alchemy of mischief.

⁋ For most of their existence, golliwogs live in a landscape of rumpled bedclothes.

⁋ A golliwog and a doll within the warm secrecy of a toy-cupboard.

⁋ Golliwogs believe that the Sun is black. He is the Lord of Midnight who pours coolness upon the Earth.

⁋ Blow out the candle, and your golliwog will disappear.

⁋ A golliwog in the house is an invitation to blackguardry.

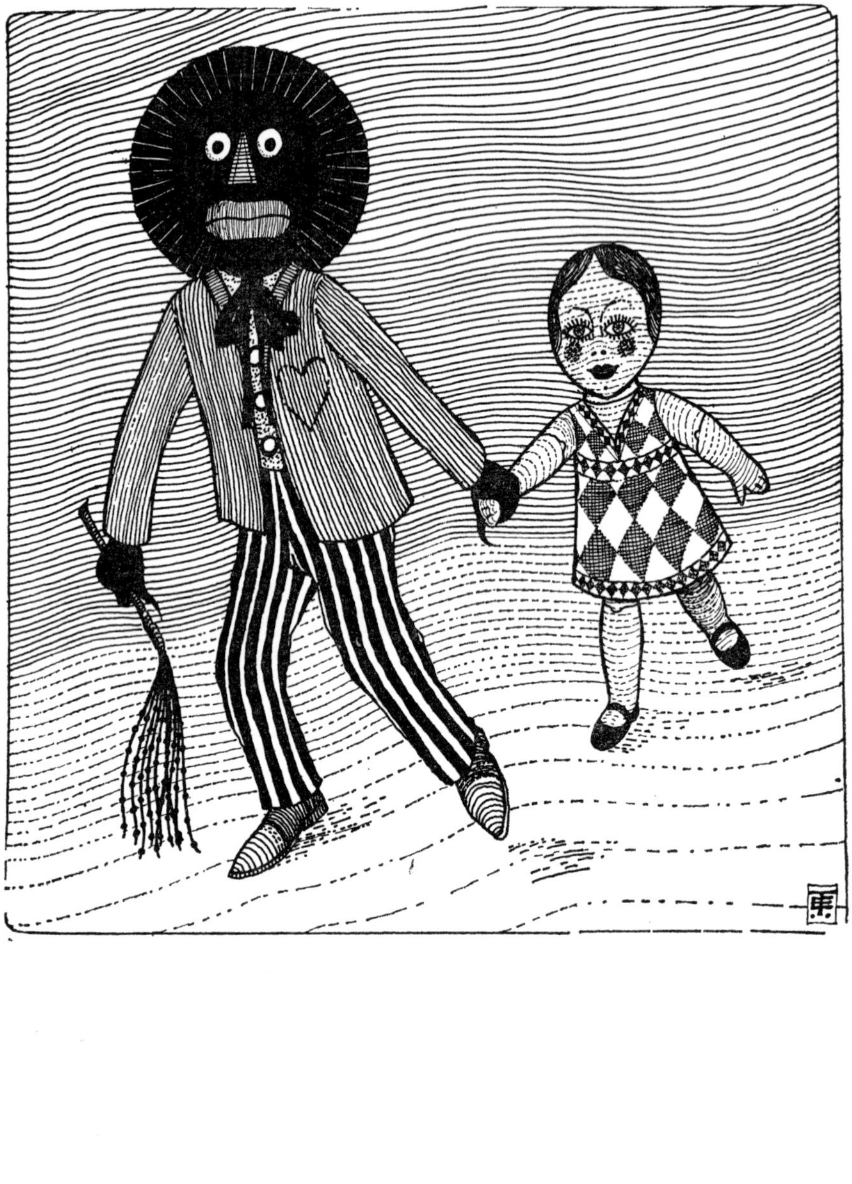

## DEVOTIONS

Bella repaired to the chantry and fumed its crepuscular arches with pious incense.

'*All' armi, Garibaldi!*' she whispered. 'Break out of your sepulchre, Redshirt, and march to my relief. Giuseppe of the falchion, Giuseppe of the drum ... lay your frozen hand on my burning brow.'

But Garibaldi slept quietly on beneath the granite cliffs of Caprera. It is doubtful whether he heard her at all.

# WINDOWS

We normally disregard our windows with criminal negligence, looking *through* them but seldom *at* them.

❡ We clean them, but only in order to make them less noticeable.

❡ A window is invisibility framed.

❡ Frosted panes and leadings of stained glass are not true windows.

❡ A true window is an eye for wind and light.

❡ It is a short corridor through which light and sight pass unimpeded.

❡ Who would be a window? It performs a thankless duty.

❡ Your windowpane was once sand; the sand was once rock; the rock was once primal slag; the slag was once solar fire ... The rest is in the eye of God.

During Christmas's year in his room, the Window assumed an importance out of all proportion to its size. It was made up of four diamonds held apart by a kiss.

In the daytime Christmas viewed the world from the inside of the Room. By night he viewed the Room from the outside world. In either case the view was the same.

He found no need to record his night-time viewing, since all he saw was familiar and unchanging. The urge to record his daytime viewing was certainly there, at all times, but every time he opened his Diary in the hush of evening he found today's observances already recorded – and tomorrow's as well. Had he not possessed a remarkably bad memory, life would have lacked spice entirely.

## THE DIARY ENTRY OF THE LAST DAY IN THE ROOM

7.30 a.m. My frosted eyes look at the clear Window. The distance is not empty, yet neither is it full. As the sun rises the mists take fright and hurry away towards November cities, leaving unclothed a sombre edifice. It is about half-a-mile away; I have known it more distant. It is a Palace of alarming dimensions, intricate in shape, and surrounded by an army of well-drilled fir trees. Amid the tedious green are a few urgent patches of festive colour. I see also the occasional blink of candles, and wonder if it is my birthday. Gifts begin to arrive from friends and relations of whom I have never heard.

Though there is no wind, the fir trees sway and dip constantly.

8.20 a.m. From the back door of the Palace a close-ranked platoon emerges and hacks a path through the forest to the Northern demarcation. Are they warriors, or lumbermen? It is impossible to tell from here. The metallic gleamings could come either from halberds or axes. The figures disappear behind the hedge. Squeals of delight and groans of pain come faintly to my ears, but no further activity, human or divine, is to be seen.

8.55 a.m. I fancy I espy a tiny figure moving along the ramparts of the Palace. It is so small that if I reached out I could pick it up and pocket it without anybody noticing. As it moves, a tiny flash of light blooms, from time to time, like a snowflake in lamplight. A ring or a brooch, perhaps, deftly stealing sunlight. The flashes are not harsh, threatening, metallic, like the implements of the platoon; they are soft, feminine, alluring, like the scintillations of jewellery. Now they assume the frequency of a signal code. I receive the message without comprehension, and file it away in the dark drawer of my soul.

9.00 a.m. The figure disappears. I turn from the Window and attend to my mechanical orchestra, dusting the gaudy figures with a small hand-bellows. The cymbals of the rearmost bandsman are ill-aligned and do not collide cleanly. I wind the mechanism, counting the turns meticulously. Up goes the switch, and I hear again the tinny strains of a martial air. The impudent sounds build to a frenzy, and, at the climax, the left arm of the cymbalist breaks off and clatters to the platform. When the music ends, my fingers extricate the limb from among the little striped legs. They lift it to my mouth, which eats it obediently. Poison! Always poison!

I brush the crumbs from my chin, and fish from the cupboard a small sign to hang on the orchestra switch.

> OUT
> OF
> ORDER

10.15 a.m. A grey, astringent rain falls from the leaden sky, and a wall of stone-coloured mist builds itself around the Room.

10.30–11.15 a.m. I mix my palette and rapidly execute four self-portraits revealing different contours of my personality.

11.15 a.m.–2.00 p.m. I stand by the Window, wondering where the Palace has gone. I can see the fir trees, but dare not look at them for long. The fiery eyes of wolves and lynxes are kindling.

The platoon reappears to commence the assault upon the forest. Hacking and lopping, it denudes the estate, and, with the aid of the wild beasts, drags away the helpless trees. Great clouds of evicted birds darken the sky.

2.00–4.45 p.m. For the rest of the afternoon, I busy myself about the Room. How smooth these pipes are; these augmentary tubes and flues which here and there invade the Room. My fingers measure and caress these bland obtrusions with erotic skill, sensing the vast intermural pattern of which they are outcroppings. I hear the sibilance of fugitive creatures – gas, quicksilver, refuse, and mice – escaping along these hidden avenues. On a ludicrous impulse, I begin to dismantle chosen areas of the walls, and then apply a carefully selected ear to the uncovered pipes. I hear the strong voice of liberty mocking my captive dreams.

4.45–6.00 p.m. The view from the Window elicits tears of grief and rage. My Factory is in sight again, and in a pother of smoky travail. It is bigger, now, than ever before, looking as though it might, at

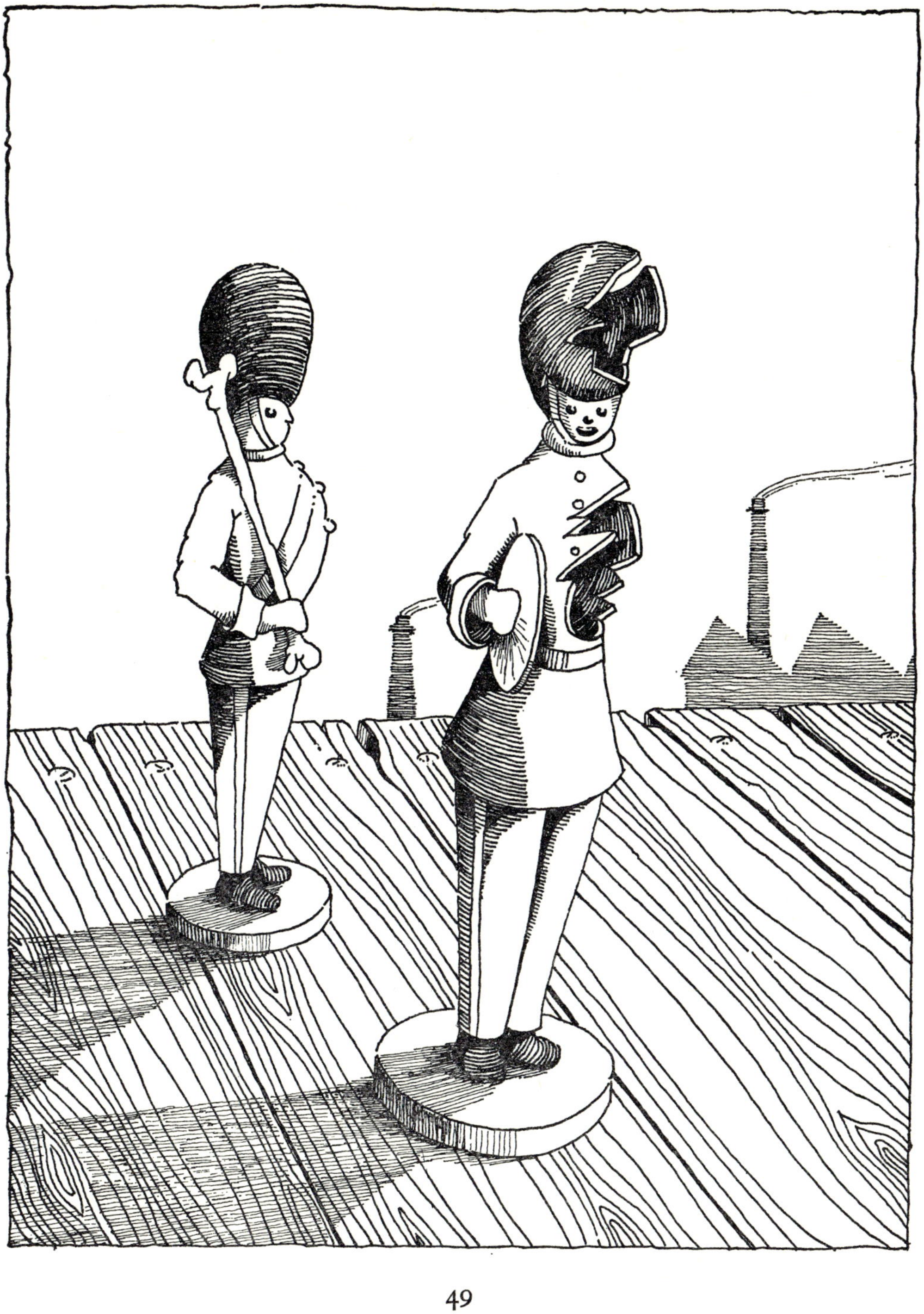

any moment, gulp down my tasty Room. Why does it keep coming back to taunt me with mementoes of my former proprietorship. I fume inwardly at the beauty of its russet chimneys with their nubiferous plumes. Always I have loved the chimneys most; those impeccable edifacts whose upstretched throats pattern the lazy sky with the dark breath of honest industry. They are the steeples of an ebullient religion whose prayers are visible to all.

My father was a steeplejack, my mother a cat-burglar. From them I have inherited two sterling traits – a low rapacity and a head for heights. But how can I exercise these faculties, imprisoned in this isolated cubicle. How I envy the truant smoke escaping so facilely from the gullets of those brick-lined flues to float in freedom across the heavens.

Dusk falls, and the Factory gradually fades from sight.

6.00 p.m. My grandfather clock intones the hour with senile uncertainty, and I note with vague alarm that the twilight is being assisted to darken the Room by a vaporous smoke. Mephitic exhalations are rising through cracks in the floor, and, already, many of my darling possessions are obscured by the murk. I stumble from corner to corner frantically checking my treasures by touch. This process has to be recommenced again and again as I lose count with typical carelessness. Eventually the smoke drugs me into a narcotic trance. I grope my way to the valuable brass bed, and sink into the mattress and oblivion.

In my dream the clocks of distant towns strike the hour of seven. I stand at the porthole of a lazily drifting ship, viewing the lofty cliffs of an alien coast. The very instability of the land is beguiling. Perhaps it enshrines a benison unglimpsed, in dream, or in dream within dream.

The ship is sailing Southward, for, as I watch, the dusk thickens, and the sun sinks towards the horizon, lowered to its grave in a coffin of cloud. Ragged bats twitter their requiem, like black priests celebrating the interment of Sol.

I turn back into the cabin, discovering it to be a nautical version of my own little Room. Climbing into the hammock I swing into wakefulness.

8.15 p.m. I begin a furious labour. Hodding bricks and stones from the ruined walls, I build a round, wide-throated chimney at the centre of the floor. As I complete it the first wisps of smoke curl and writhe from its sooty rim.

I pause beside my handiwork and glance at the Window. To my dismay it is aglow with sunlight, none of which penetrates into the recesses of the Room. Furthermore, it is visibly if slightly changing shape. It is a window no longer. Now it is an island, lapped by surging tides of darkness. Above the rage of the wind I hear the mewing of homeless arctic seabirds.

'Intersol! Intersol!' they seem to cry.

Gathering my multifarious effects into a hessian sack, I don the scarlet playsuit which my mother so grudgingly sewed for me long ago, and swing my booted leg over the chimney's lip.

# THE ROOM ABANDONED

THUS, at a new stage of self-awareness, Christmas began his escape from the prison of his tenth year into the grimy freedom of his eleventh. As the excited fugitive disappeared down the chimney the light of the enisled Window was extinguished and bailiff shadows occupied the Room. In the pipes and flues invisible travellers still chirped, muttered, and groaned.

## CHIMNEYS

⁋ Industrious man cannot claim to have invented chimneys. He borrowed the principle from nature.
⁋ Volcanoes are the world's most beautiful chimneys.
⁋ Blessed are they who inhabit the fissures of the earth.
⁋ They shall breathe the fumes of subterranean prayer.
⁋ Chimneystacks or minarets ... steeplejacks or muezzins ... take your choice.
⁋ Above the end of every street looms the reeking stack that haunts the dreams of children.
⁋ 'Round chimneys are better than square ones' (Old Technical Manual).
⁋ Never deprive a chimney of its lightning-rod.
⁋ 'Therefore shall they be as the morning cloud, and as the early dew that passeth away, as the chaff that is driven with the whirlwind out of the floor, and as the smoke out of the chimney' (Hosea xiii 3).

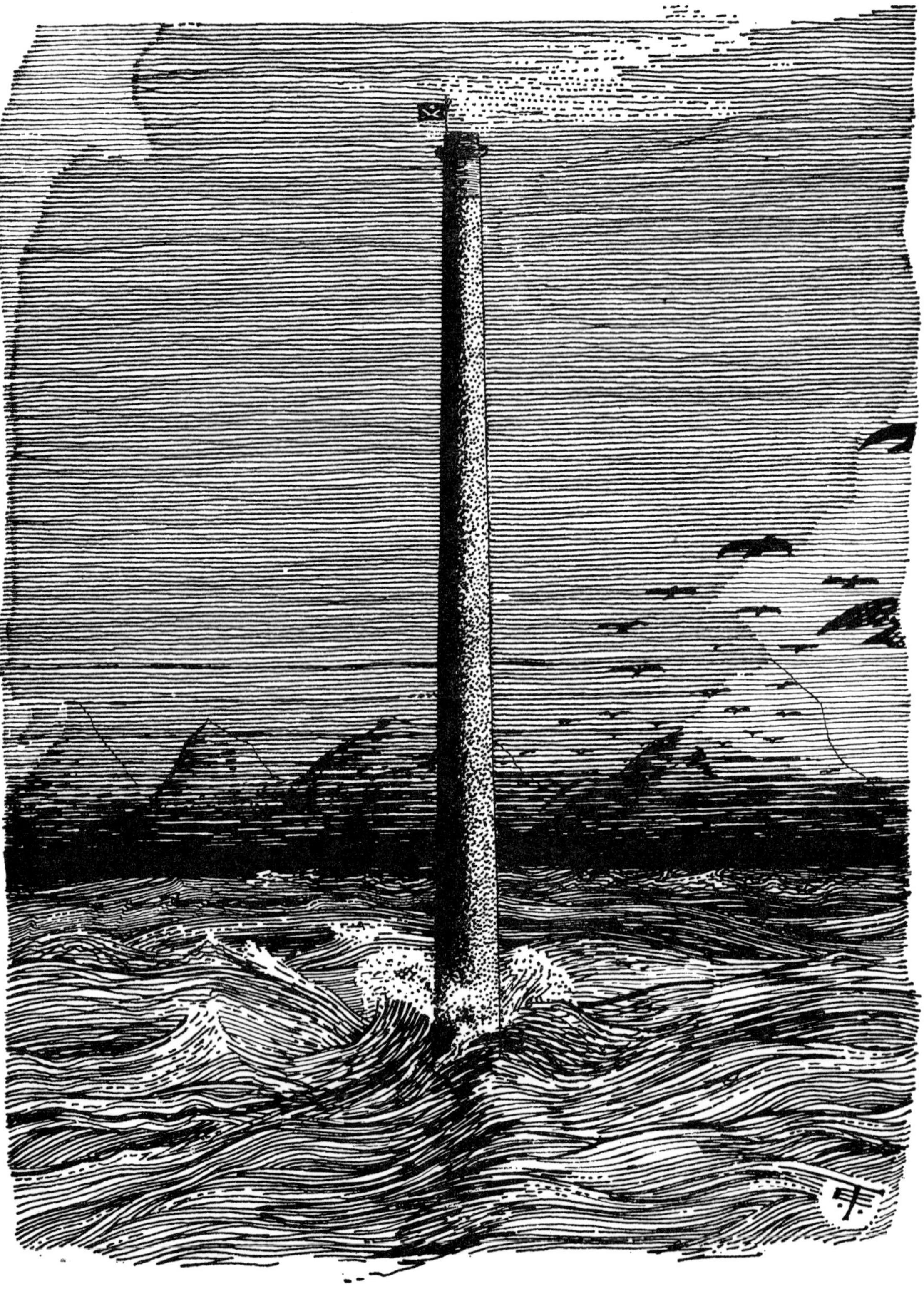

⁋ Not even snow glistens more brightly than the white of a chimneysweep's eye.
⁋ Christmas built chimneys of smoke.
⁋ Religion is the chimney of our aspirations. Far above us God sniffs the odour of our burnt offerings.
⁋ Christmas built his chimney according to plans and instructions stolen from Vulcan.
⁋ Nobody knows who Vulcan stole them from.
⁋ Christmas's construction was the epitome of chimneytude.
⁋ It reeked to suit a variety of tastes and moods: coalsmoke, woodsmoke, turfsmoke, cowpatsmoke, tallowsmoke, oilsmoke, papersmoke, ragsmoke, sacrificial smoke, the smoke of banned books, and the steams of boiling and basting.
⁋ It was a homely chimney. Bats, snails, and crickets hunted happily in its fumescent spaces.
⁋ The interior of the chimney was equipped with ladders of hemp, leather, silk, whalebone, wood, and iron. It also boasted occasional stairways, chutes, tightropes, and bridges.
⁋ Passages of varying degrees of secrecy provided egress from the chimney at several fortuitous points.
⁋ Some passages were linked to caverns, others to large cellars, and yet others to chimneys of lesser importance.
⁋ On certain occasions, when Christmas was exploring the passages and the regions into which they led, he lost his chimney and was compelled to build another before he was free to proceed upon his way.
⁋ Christmas found his keenest happiness in the chimney. It brought to his life a new simplicity of purpose.
⁋ Chimneymoss is toothsome fare.

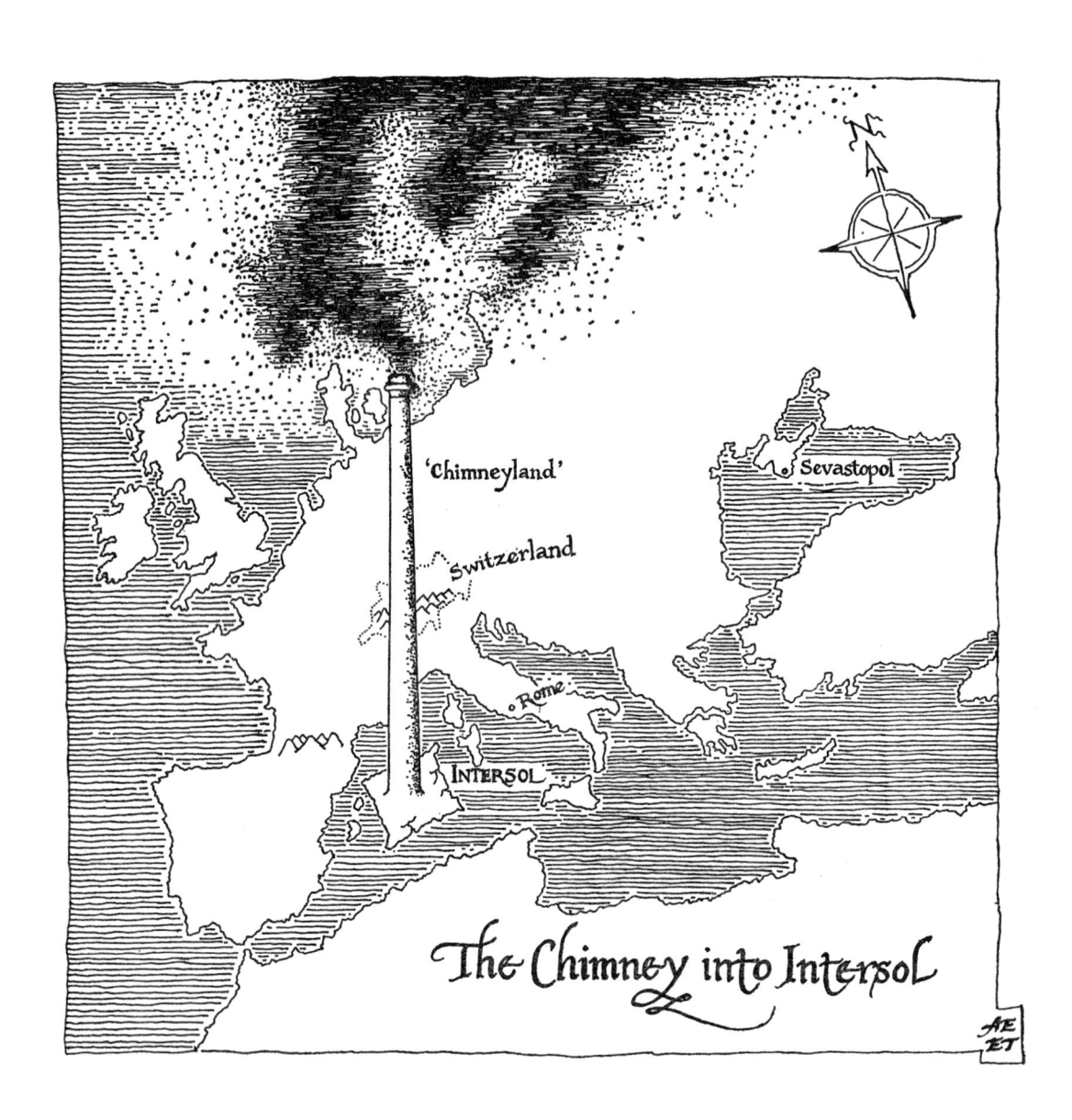

*The Chimney into Intersol*

# HOCUS POCUS

A DECEITFUL SIDE-ROAD led Christmas into southern Scandinavia. He captivated the simple folk of the towns with his pleasantries, but soon began to suspect that they had grown wary of his presence. Approaching a village new to him, he became aware that leading citizens were conferring together against him, and that wicked constabulary were lying in wait. Taking out a small lacy handkerchief he threw it idly over the muttering hamlet, and then whipped it away with lightning speed. The village had vanished. He tossed the handkerchief into his sack and strode on.

Further on, he met the inhabitants of a notable town armed with staves and brickbats. He donned a mask of innocence and, in answer to their inquiry after some approaching felon, directed them up a tapering side-road. After the band of animated figures had dwindled into the distance, he plucked up the entire road and secreted it in a capacious pocket inside his cloak. Continuing to the town he ransacked the homes and churches without interference.

He sat in the snow like a miser, sifting his swag. Without warning, a band of unruly children, accompanied by sharp-toothed pets, surged towards him, snarling with envy. But they were not quick enough. The hooded thief scooped the booty into his sack, and disappeared into the dark cave which was always close at hand.

Swiftly losing his pursuers in a maze of tunnels he regained the main shaft and resumed his earnest descent.

# SERVICES

The resourceful Gamin knew that there were, as yet, many rewarding levels of experience to explore. He was heartened to discover that the Chimney was neatly integrated with the pipe-system of his forsaken Room. Many of those metallic tubes made contact with the principle flue. They enabled him to gain intelligence about the higher reaches, and thus he was reassured against the possibility of pursuit. In addition, the pipes supplied him with needful elements of sustenance, ablution, stimulation, narcosis, warmth, and lubrication for body and mind. Life can be rich and satisfying even in a chimney.

ower down, the inlets and outlets were larger and more primitive — caves, rocky passages, and echoing potholes. Very few of these were inhabited, and then only by crickets or tribes of blind musicians. On the eve of his fifteenth birthday, Christmas entered a promising cavern and, after a series of minor adventures, emerged blacker and craftier than ever in the industrial kingdom of Germany.

His first sight of Germany caused him to weep bitter, icy tears. It needed only casual scrutiny to convince him that this was a land far-famed for its chimneys tall and short. It was a Black Forest of chimneys, and the sun had long since given up hope of penetrating the twilight of its smoky pall.

In those areas of the world to which it exported its staple product, Germany was known as Chimneyland.

Once he had subjugated his envy, Christmas found Chimneyland a place of signal enlightenment. Eavesdropping upon the councils of the Chimneyfactors, grateful heirs of an ancient craft, he learned many a dusty secret, and filched sheaves of valuable handbooks and blueprints.

Wandering over the huddled roofs and scaling the loftiest and dizziest stacks, never once relinquishing his hold on the sack, he enhanced his climbing skills. Nor did he forget his more dubious expertise. The homes and mills of Chimneyland unwittingly contributed much to his bulging hoard.

## SWITZERLAND

Christmas began to yearn for the slimy walls and dank fumes of his own precipitous flue. Leaving Chimneyland he clambered aimlessly down through his sixteenth and seventeenth years. These differed from one another only as starfall differs from snowshine. By the time he reached Switzerland he was well into his eighteenth year and the stubble was white on his rosy cheek.

The advent of Christmas in Switzerland went unnoticed at first. He subsisted for a time on acts of petty larceny, but he was soon inspired to more impressive infamies. He preached the gospel of skulduggery to believer and unbeliever alike and, smiling his enchanting smile, as the first frosty whiskers of manhood curled round his lips, he sucked Switzerland dry. There was no available item of value which did not become food for his omnivorous sack. He was a one-man crime-wave.

The shadow of penury fell across the land, and the seams of the great sack became remarkably strained. Yet, Christmas's covetousness decreased not a whit.

Resting in his robber's lair, Christmas suddenly recalled a childhood companion. Answering an urge to confirm the fact of his notoriety, he raided the sack and seized the Diary. He opened it at random, and read on avidly.

# DECEMBER 19th

*I am now about to consult six pages from my diary*

12.15 AM

12.19 AM

2.45 PM

10.08 PM

# DECEMBER 20th

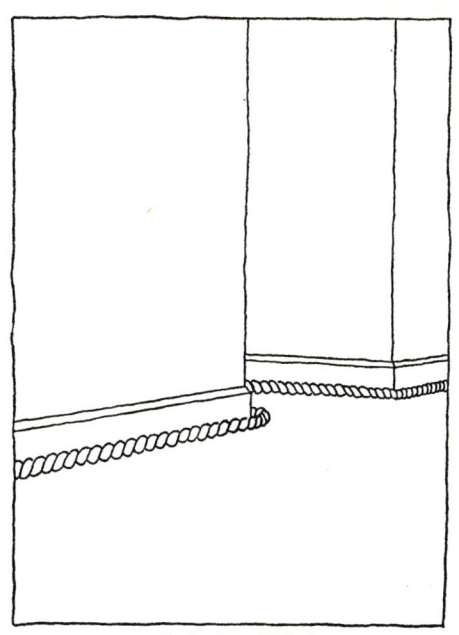

11.13 PM

11.16 PM

11.45 PM

11.47 PM

# DECEMBER 21st

8.25 AM

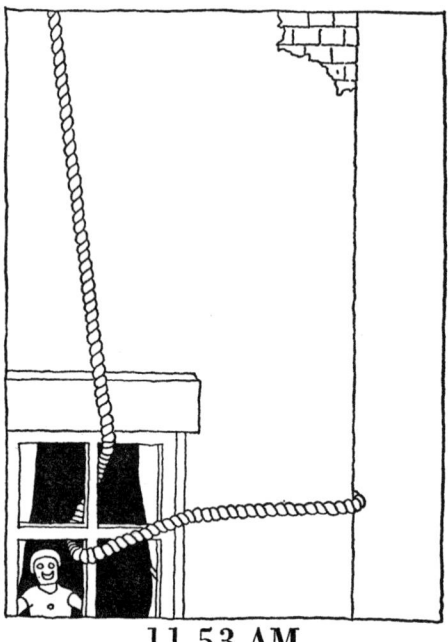

11.53 AM

9.08 PM

11.57 PM

# DECEMBER 22nd

12.05 AM

12.10 AM

1.10 AM

11.59 PM

# DECEMBER 23rd

2.45 AM

11.58 AM

12.10 PM

5.05 PM

# DECEMBER 24th

10.15 PM

10.25 PM

11.05 PM

12.00 PM

# THE BIRTHDAY BOX

A twentieth birthday in Switzerland is everyone's dream of paradise. Christmas basked in the glow of self-admiration and quaffed the brimming cup of excess. Early in the morning an enigmatic parcel arrived mysteriously from who-knows-where. The parcel lay unheeded in the felicitous hugger-mugger, and when, in the purple hush of evening, Christmas unwrapped it, he discovered a small, square box, mildewed and mottled with irregular patches of damp. On its level top lay a weird dusting of snow.

Christmas gazed at this box for an unreasonable length of time. Why did it remind him so much of a window? Why did he recall the thin complaint of the stormy petrel? Why did Pandora-like warnings hiss in the still shadows of his parlour?

Murdering circumspection with a single thrust, he snatched the lid from the box and peered inside. It was quite empty. But out of the interior there rose a poignant, taunting perfume which set his pulses thudding like a factory machine.

He glanced at the Portrait on the wall. The Lady's expression did not alter.

Things eventually grew too hot for Christmas in Switzerland. Realizing that the forces of rectitude were closing in, he packed quickly, and left without paying his bills. His faithful escape-route lay at hand, and he took to its homely spaces without delay.

In the following months he achieved the Sack of Avignon, the Crucifixion of Genoa, and the Rape of Nice. The bulk of Europe's treasures were now his, and his name became a byword for turpitude. His face bore the ravages of greed, his thews stiffened with exertion. He began to wonder if the game was worth the candle.

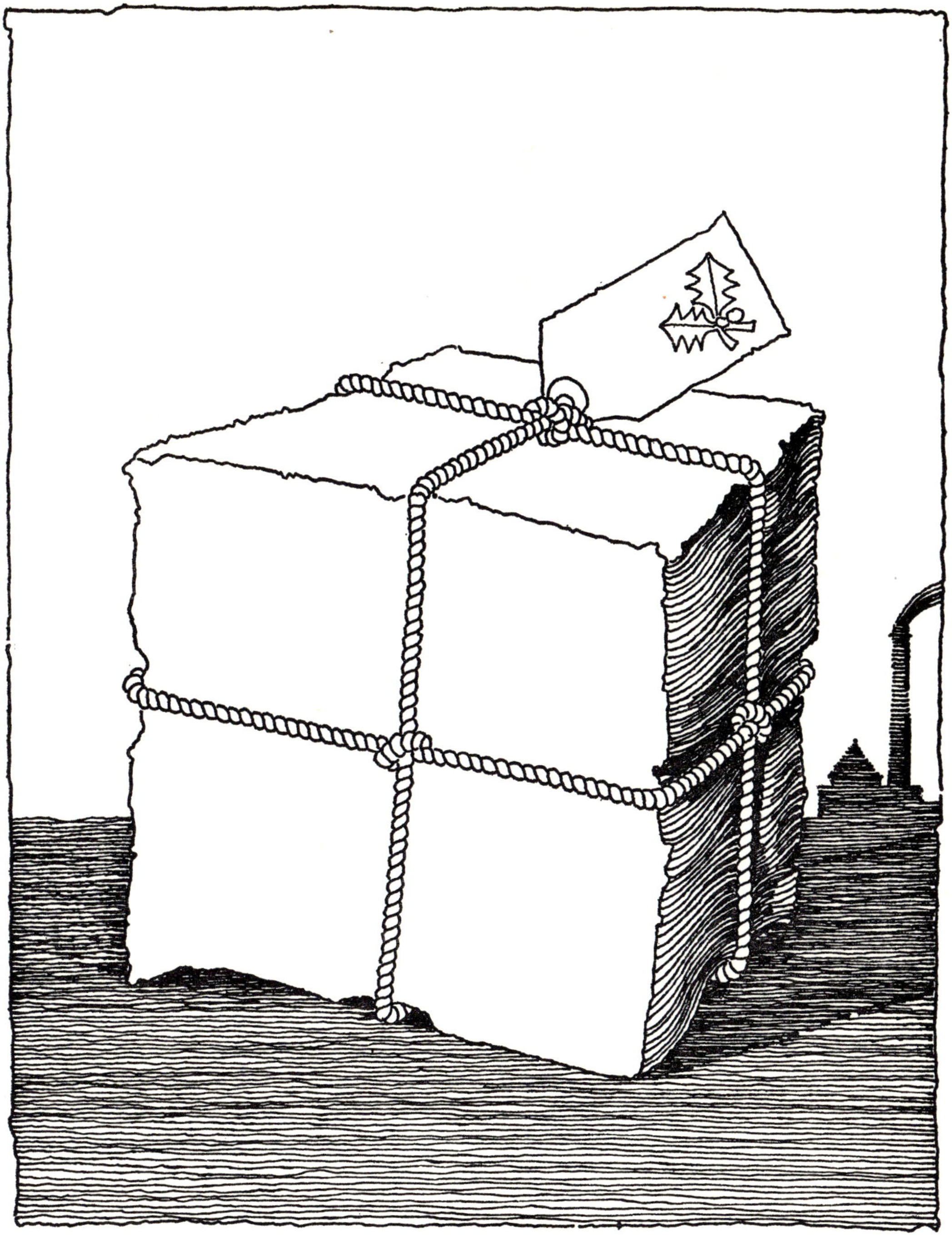

# THE END OF THE CENTURY

LATE IN 1899 he stumbled through a particularly fusty adit and ended up in a boxlike cave furnished as an office and adorned with trade-calendars, regulations-charts, and sporting-prints. He viewed the enclosure with distaste, and would have turned back had he not detected a faint, congenial odour. The perfume wafted to his nostrils through the office-cave was identical with the perfume which had emanated from the mysterious gift-box.

Whirling round with narrowed eyes, he conned the room, and marked with a thrill of recognition a picture hitherto unnoticed ... a cheap but clever copy of his Portrait of a Beautiful Lady. Incensed by the mockery, Christmas snatched up a paperweight to shy, but a slight movement of the image checked him.

It was not a picture after all ... it was a window!

His heart raced as he peered out of the simple frame across the tips of fir trees, at the casement from which the living face of his ideal stared back. A spiderthread of understanding linked his eyes with hers. He had no inkling of the cunning web this exotic belle might yet weave to enmesh him. He only knew that he was looking at the incarnation of childhood's dream, the consummation of manhood's avarice.

He gazed at her till darkness fell. Somewhere near at hand a siren howled with wolflike finality.

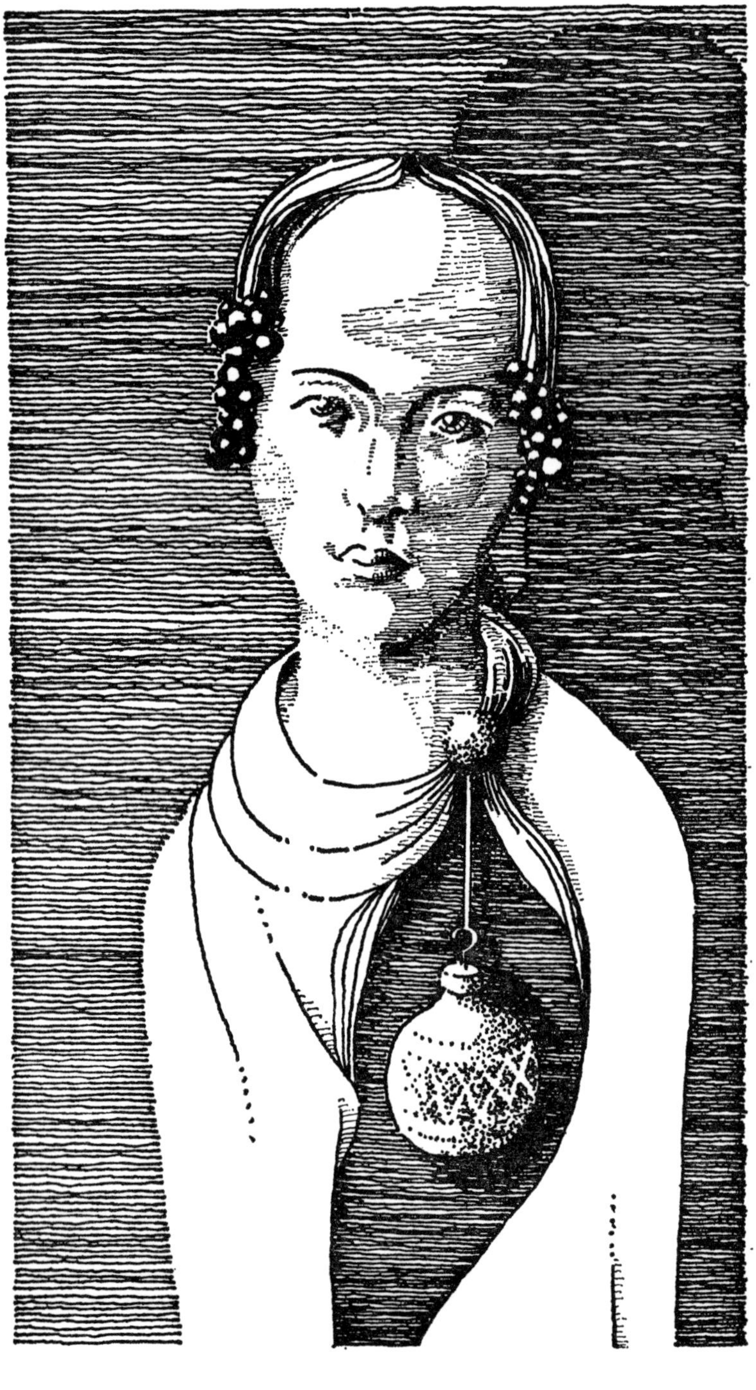

# TUNNELS

THE CHIMNEY is a vertical tunnel.
⁋ Obelisks are recalcitrant tunnels.
⁋ Bella ordered her seamstress to install two tunnels in a new garment. When this was accomplished, she slid her arms into them.
⁋ She also ordered her engineers to fill in a tunnel and then to remove its mountain. The outcome was a fine cylindrical wall.
⁋ Christmas was prince of the subterranean ways.
⁋ He mapped most carefully the many tunnels of the human body.
⁋ Caverns are the gullets of hungry mountains.
⁋ Night is the tunnel between today and tomorrow.
⁋ Mole, rabbit, earthworm, deathwatch beetle, kingfisher, and trap-door spider – our most esoteric sappers.
⁋ Bella hated the Tunnel of Love.
⁋ Christmas nurtured his love of tunnels.
⁋ It was a dark, narrow, deeply buried emotion, which led to his eventual ruin.
⁋ Womb and tomb: the tunnels of birth and death.
⁋ A famous cardsharp won a small, valuable tunnel from Bella by trumping her Queen of Hearts with the King of Spades.
⁋ Bella kept the Ace up her sleeve.

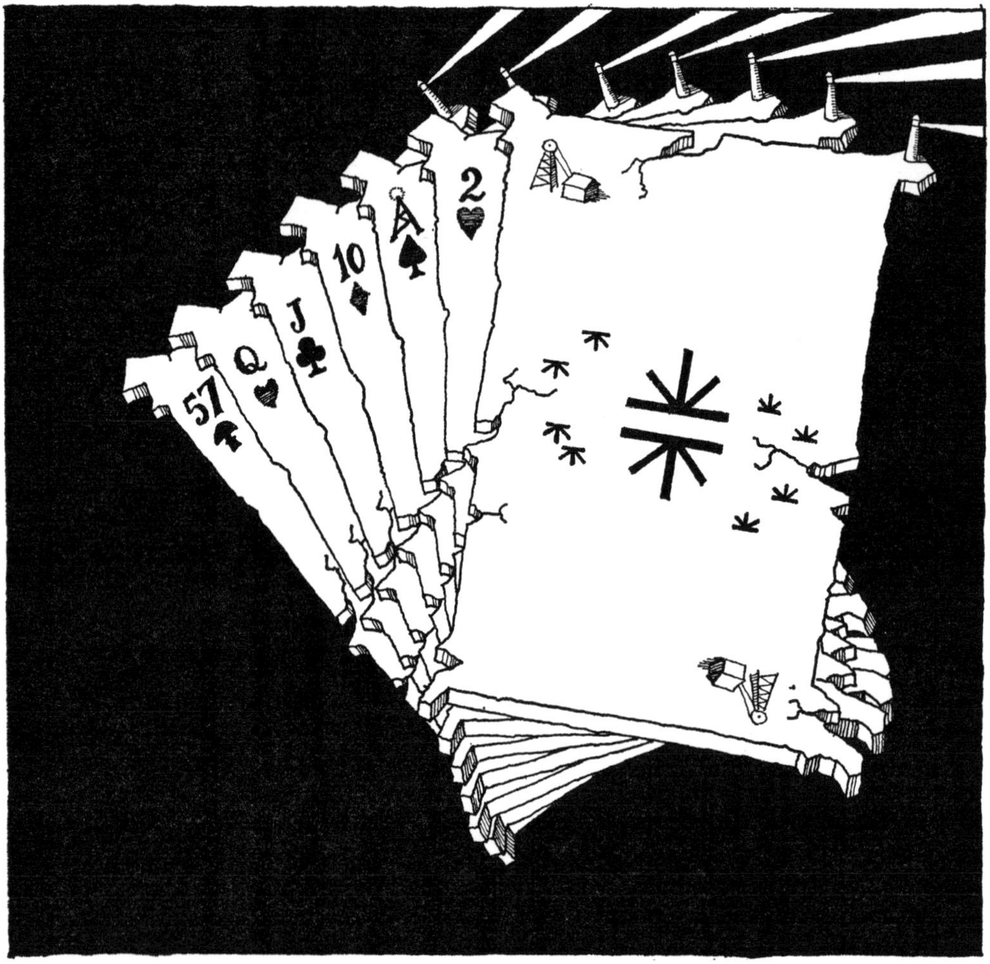
57
Q
J
10
A
2

# CONCATENATIONS

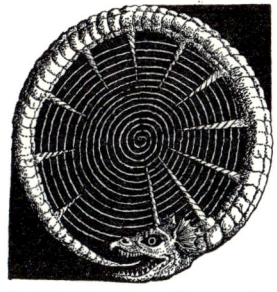

UROBOROS, the serpent that swallows its own tail, becomes the wheel of a universal appetite.

⁋ Lovers holding hands ape the cannibal banquet of the worm.

⁋ The spade of dawn exposes sleepers like night-buried roots.

⁋ Christmas dispatched an anonymous chain-letter which returned to him by freak chance, some years later, unread and unaugmented.

⁋ Tight-chain-walkers in suits of chequered armour.

⁋ Bella threaded a necklet of mercury globules.

⁋ The children of the pioneers face outward in their ring-games.

⁋ The point at which stalactite meets stalagmite is the perfect nemesis.

⁋ Christmas espoused the religion of nature. Frog-spawn was his rosary.

# A HOME-MADE ROOM

Bella's miniscule cyclorama still vexed her like a riddle. She had dragged it from a forgotten chest on a sultry day, and had read again the cursory admonition:

> AFFIX FACTORY,
> ROOM, OR
> STREET HEREON

Here was the pointer to the model's basic wrongness. Plainly, three parts were lacking, yet only two empty sites were available. She had once possessed the Factory and the Street, but where was the Room? Mesmerized by desire's passing hand, she resolved to be deprived no longer of the ultimate delight. At the exact centre of her echoing nursery, she set to and, with her own translucent hands, built and furnished a Room in the precise likeness of the one she had never seen but often imagined.

Some inexplicable urge prompted her to set at the centre a cosy hearth and chimneypiece. She instantly kindled a modest fire, and sat with glowing pride watching the upward trickle of smoke.

In this secret asylum she lived out her choicest dream of Lilliputian disorder. Many were her delicious shudders as she crouched in the Room listening to the howl of the blizzard and the tattoo of the hailstorm threatening the rickety ceiling and flimsy walls.

Here she lapped her harpoon to the sharpness of a stiletto, and baited her fish-hooks with succulent meats. Here she planned her audacious hunting and heard, in anticipation, the grunt and bark of bear and seal across the immeasurable icy vicinage beyond the door.

Her dreams became enmeshed in the wallpaper's gaudy tangle, as if in the steamy intimacy of a jungle. She felt as if the Northern settlement was the only home she had ever known. This was one of the most spellbound afternoons of her short but ineffably beautiful life.

## THE RED WORKER

At the window, Bella looked out at bunched and brooding clouds and heard the far-off mutter of thunder. A truant flash of lightning illumined the harsh landscape, and there, silhouetted against the sky, she saw the spectral image of a long-lost well-remembered friend. The years peeled back as she recognized the Factory . . . recognized it, even though it was transformed by the years. It was vast and virile, and filled the horizon; it moaned, belched, and

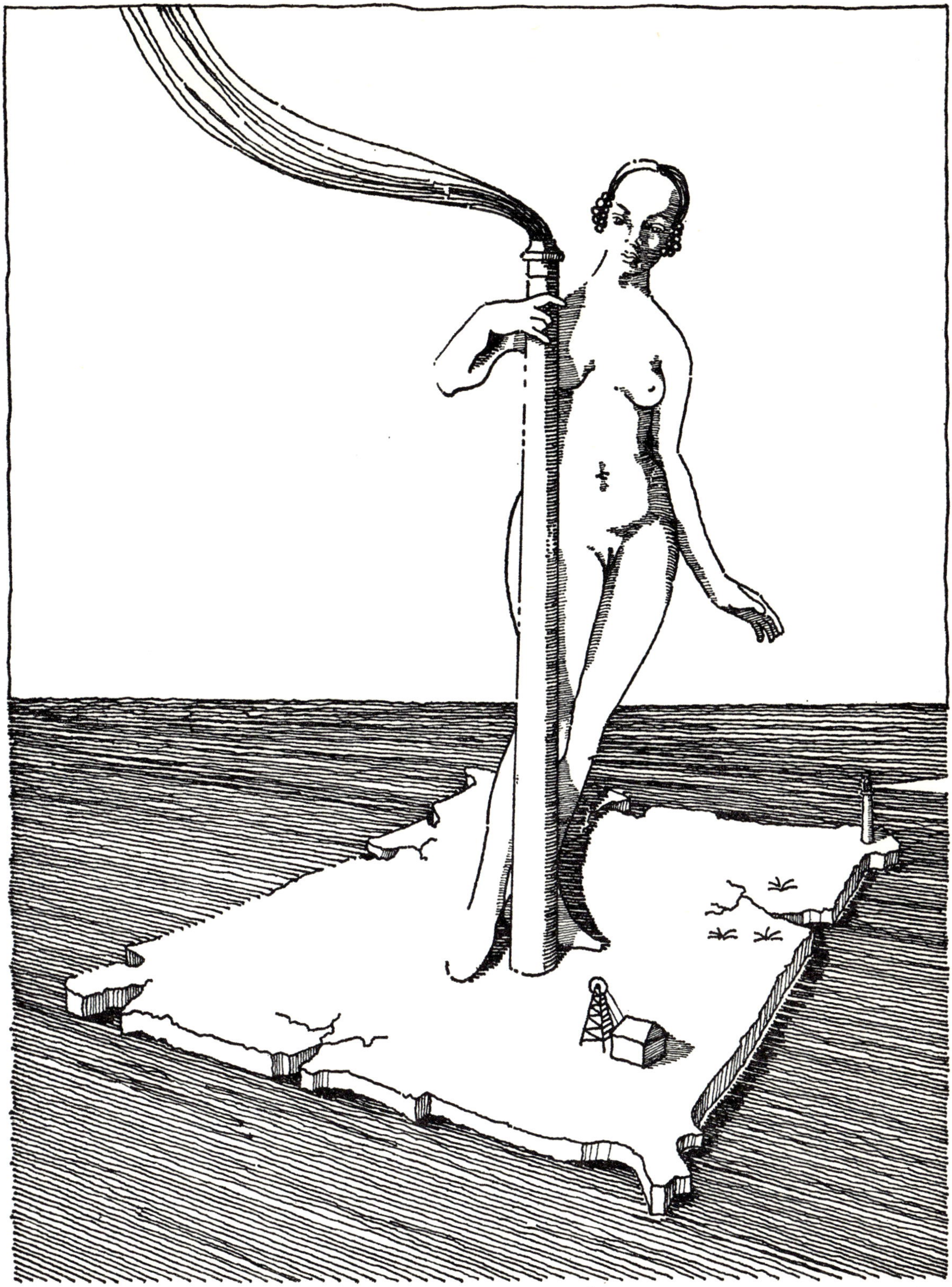

clanked in unretarded motion; and, best of all, it was within easy reach.

Sweetness oozed from the honeycomb of Bella's brain as she watched the comings and goings of a maddeningly familiar boyish figure. Diminutive and agile, he scrambled up ladders, scurried across gantries, and emerged from gateways to load waiting drays with well-wrapped oddities.

For all the lusty turmoil of the Factory, this youngster appeared to be its sole employee.

In following days, Bella embraced the life of an anchoress, praying to her palefaced idols and hurling shrill maledictions at Intersol, that claustral box of sadness. Indeed, for her Intersol ceased to exist. Reality was the Room, the Window, and the boundless promise of the frozen North. She somersaulted backwards into the madness of youth.

Now she had space to dream in, and most of her dreams were of the lissome factory-hand. She followed his industrious career, from his smooth-jowled apprenticeship to his stubbly manhood. The images flickered uncertainly, but it seemed that eventually he seized control of the Factory and imposed a new regime, a smoky empire of which he alone was judge and lord.

Bella saw him seated in his office poring over ponderous ledgers and riddling schedules. This seemed orderly enough, and yet she suspected that his motives were hardly those of an honest manager. They were closer to those of a thief rifling a strongbox. Rapacious hungers gleamed candlelike in his narrow eyes.

For another thing, he was curiously uniformed for one bound by workaday concerns. The naked bulb of the office light shone on the vivid fabric adorning his limbs. Bella tittered her unbelief. Whoever heard of red overalls?

Red!

Bella's heart leapt, and rebel dreams raced to man the barricades of speculation. Was the crystallization of her wintry hopes at hand? Was this the red-garbed liberator who would bedeck her life with the icicles of joy?

In that identical moment, the red worker strode purposefully to the office window, and, as he looked out, their eyes met in violent communion.

One thing led to another, and, in no time at all, Bella and Christmas began to communicate by other means.

# LETTERS

'OTABELLA, my pretty silver wheel,' wrote Christmas, 'I want you to spin the fortunes of my journeys, and carry me hither and thither with the speed of starlight. There are so many places to go, so many sights to see!'

'Warden of the Snow, Rubicotta,' responded Bella, 'I feel already the blizzard of your beard. Red-garbed, white-haired, woolly-mittened, jack-booted, sack-bearing, chimney-creeping, kindly burglar, you are my Garibaldi sprung from the grave.'

'The laggard postman is no friend of lovers,' wrote Christmas. 'Enough of paltry scribblings! I shall dispatch myself, a living letter, for you to open and read. Be ready!'

'Fly down, gaudy robin, and perch on my finger,' implored Bella. 'Sing me the thin song of winter. If you want me to believe in you, do not disappoint me or disregard my final request.'

# BEDTIME

Bella sealed up her last letter as she sat by the fire conjuring her lover's portrait in the flames. She committed the urgent missive to the ascending smoke, and strove to cultivate a patience adequate to her years. Then she looked out at the Factory window which had hitherto framed that rosy face. The space was empty.

And so were the days that followed.

In dishabille, distrait and solitary, Bella left the Room and wandered through the halls and arcades of the December Palace. It was a return to a drab world after a journey to the mouth of Aladdin's Grotto and a tantalizing glimpse of the riches within. Adventure gave way to humdrum routine. She did little more than allay the pangs of her own hunger or that of her wolves, weed the garden, dust the furniture, wind the clocks, or dismiss the handful of truculent farriers who remained in her service.

But the Room proved magnetic, and drew her back into its square confines . . .

A white hush possessed the Room, but this was a mere prelude. The hearth was unusually volcanic. Gusts of hot and cold air puffed fumes and sparks into the smut-laden air which magnified the Room out of all proportion. The outline of huge furniture loomed threateningly, and Bella shivered, drawing her cloak more tightly round her shoulders.

She hurried across the Room, afraid lest she be waylaid. Reaching the fireplace she paused, listening, and fancied she heard a hoarse voice calling her name. Disdaining to reply, she turned away and began to strip off her garments, strewing them without thought or care on the floor behind her. She then composed herself on the great brass bed, awaiting whatever excitements now approached.

Conspiratorial phantoms were abroad in the night. Unknown hands interfered with the sleeper's clothing. Into one of her silken stockings were thrust all sorts of rusty toys whose sharp edges snagged the delicate threads. Through the dark hours the mechanisms clicked and ground in slow, relentless motion. From the other stocking issued frothy liquids, shimmering heat, rank smells, and billowing steam. Striking through the latched Window, a rotating searchlight from the Factory found and lost her innocent features. She had the look of a ten-year-old dreaming of ice-cream.

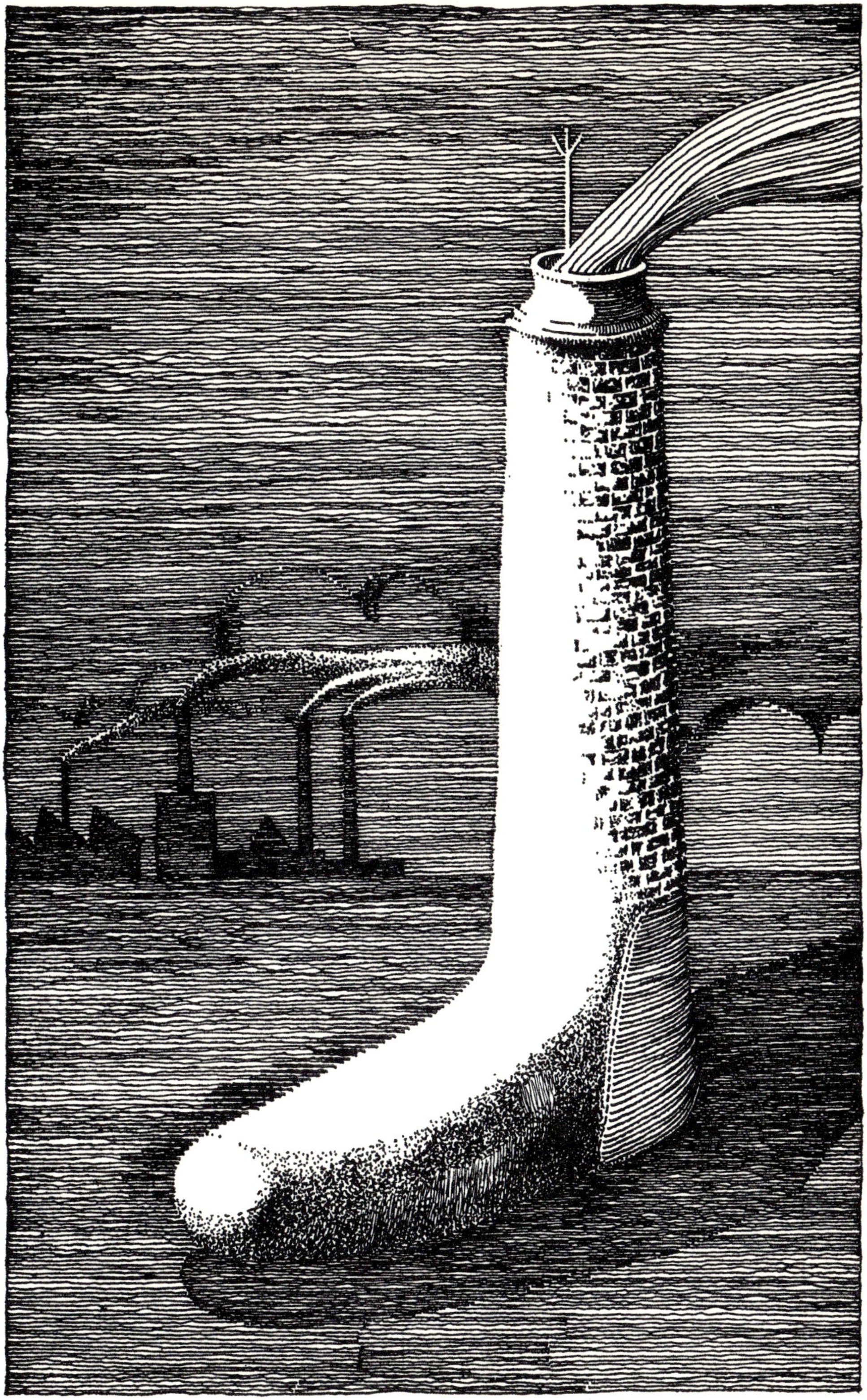

# THE COMING OF CHRISTMAS

With elephantine movements Christmas hauled himself out of the fireplace. His sack slid from his shoulder for the first time in years, and he took in great gulps of the smoky air. He was quite unaware of the sly and slender hand which emerged from the shadows of the chimney-corner and picked his half-open sack, lifting a treasure of unguessed value.

Bella, for it was she, slipped her prize into a secret place and stole away into the concealing shadows.

Leaving his sack by the cricket-beleaguered hearth Christmas hastened across the Room to the bedside. His filthy, inquiring hand crept over the blankets. The bed was empty, but still warm and fragrant.

The banging of a distant door, somewhere in the musroid world, jarred him from his reverie.

The smoke cleared, and Christmas scrutinized the Room. Amazement drove all thought of Bella from his mind. Like an awakening dreamer he stumbled about checking the old, familiar objects. Not one was missing. The Room was exactly as he had left it. Even the view from the Window was familiar ... There was the Factory in all its terrible glory, and only a spanner's-throw away.

# THE KEY

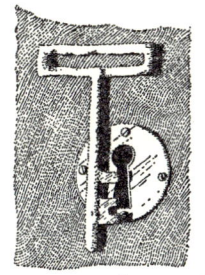

THE MYSTERY OF OPENING is enshrined in the conjunction of well-mated shapes and spaces. Less than obvious to the idealistic mind is the simple marvel of narrow orifices and shining insertions. Words of magical command, devious stratagems, violent expedients of breaking and entering ... these will always have a more beguiling attraction than the prosaic, mock-secret mechanism of key in lock.

To adapt a well-known adage: *You cannot see the wand for the wish*.

Bella had stolen the Master Key. She hung it from her neck by a silver chain and sped to the Factory. Once admitted she worked by ineluctable instinct and set in motion a co-ordinated fury of manufacture. The machinery was exactly appropriate to her venture, and with speed to satisfy the most importunate customer, she produced a silvery profusion of identical keys. Even as they rattled from the machines, she was seizing the loaded bins and scattering their contents from the Factory's grey and shabby heights to a forest of eager hands below.

## A MISTRESS OF INDUSTRY

¶ Bella ruled the factory as a priestess of gentle gimcrackery.
¶ Steam whistles called the faithless to prayer.
¶ Fires of passion turned the cog-wheels of devotion.

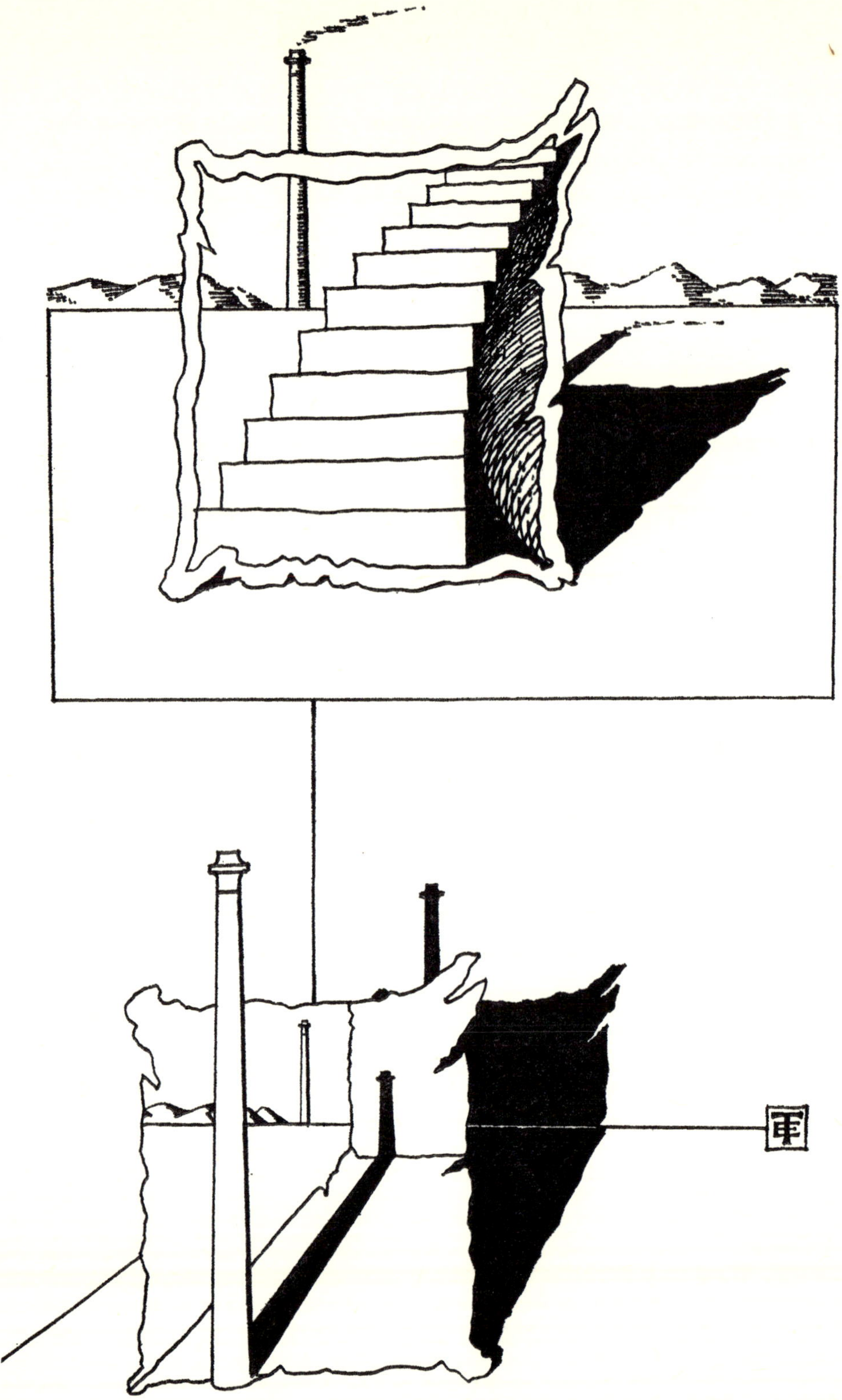

¶ Dreamflags crackled at every masthead, saluted at dawn by mechanical acolytes.
¶ Bella turned the pages of her manuals, her lips forming the shapes of interminable numerals.
¶ In the Factory basement were stored the histories of revolution and the corpses of murdered masters.
¶ Armies of workless paupers encircled the Factory day after day, chanting the slogans of defeat.
¶ Envious moneygrubbers conspired with spies and wreckers to overpower the tumultuous kingdom.
¶ Time and again, Bella had the Factory dismantled and rebuilt in secluded places, but the ingenuity of her rivals drove her to the brink of capitulation.
¶ Eventually she abandoned her hard-won domain to the legions of avarice, and took to the unseemly environs.
¶ She become lost in a labyrinth of disquiet.
¶ She asked direction of a red-cloaked stranger, but he was too intent upon his own devices to reply.

# INTO THE FACTORY

CHRISTMAS CAST a hard and longing look at his rebel possession. Again he heard the muffled clatter, smelt the acrid fumes, and felt the jarring shudder of toil.

All his senses sprang to attention. He suddenly caught sight of a shadowy figure at the rear of the dusty office, and as he stared intently the figure glided to the office window. The lovely Portrait assembled itself for his yearning gaze, and he saw his sweet ideal suspended on the dark wall. Her eyes were wide as dried-up seas, her ashen beauty implacable as cruelty.

Christmas winced.

Somewhere below, a welder's torch sputtered, throwing one half of Bella's face into sinister shadow. A jewelled hairclip glistened eloquently in her stygian tresses, but still the language of its message was beyond interpretation.

In the blue glare the entire picture assumed portentous dimensions. Jealousy stabbed Christmas. A new partnership had been established between Beauty and the Beast, taunting the white-whiskered suitor's pride.

This perverse alliance had to be subdued. Why should he be deprived of the only Woman and the only Factory in his life? He would buckle that impassive steel door beneath the urgency of his blows.

Christmas unclenched his angry fists and hefted his sack. He had covered a fair distance before a nagging suspicion stumbled into his mind. His load seemed lighter, as if some precious article were missing, and had he not been occupied with the task of weaving his way through the trees he might have been halted by unbearable doubt.

At length he confronted the steel barrier and tensed his sinews for assault, but his fist remained poised in astonished immobility. The massive door was ajar! It needed acute strategy to conquer his amazement, but urgency prevailed, and he inserted his hand into the gap. The door slid effortlessly aside on well-oiled runners, and he stepped into the noisome interior. In his excited haste he ignored a prohibition riveted lopsidedly by the entrance:

> NO
> CHILDREN
> ALLOWED

In and out of the wide-open gate workpeople hurried without let or hindrance. Joining a queue of grimy labourers, Christmas clocked in punctually at 8.30 a.m. He was blithely ignorant of the truth that the workers of the musroid world now controlled the Factory. All that concerned him, at this stage, was that the Factory was the scene of a most fascinating programme of production. Toys far bigger and more elaborate than any he had ever possessed were being fabricated pell-mell.

His mind skipped several frames of cognition. Once he had desired every toy in existence, good or bad, broken or mended. Now he realized that the Factory was all he needed. A toymaking toy! And it was his at last! . . .

Was it? . . .

Suffice it to say that he was content with his humble lot, performing his little deeds of daily skill, and cherishing the jovial camaraderie of his manly workfellows.

As he completed his stint for the day a toggle tripped in the gathering darkness of his mind. An electric flash floodlighted his disordered memory.

Christmas roved through the empty workshops, bullying timid echoes with his roar. It was only in such rest periods that his mind returned to its original purpose. Where was his lovely sweetheart? He called the name of beauty over and over, fingering the shining rosary at his belt. Fury sparked from his eyes at the thought of that usurping legion of grubby toilers defiling the cold calm of this ancient monument of his arctic childhood ... He called and called again, until the resentful echoes marshalled themselves and shrieked in frantic retaliation, their abuse resolving itself into a hooter's peremptory summons.

Back at his office, Christmas smiled dreamily as he hung a neat and homely sign above his desk:

> SILENCE

Laborious preoccupation herded all thoughts of Bella into his mind's nethermost pen.

He ticked through the many-volumed payroll and grunted his distaste. Every name on the list indicated a professional agitator. Was Bella an agitator too? He slammed the office door behind him and ranged the corridors, examining every workroom and store in an effort to find her hidyhole. His search of the Factory could not have been more thorough. No doubt of it, the sparrow had flown.

A footsore Christmas entered the canteen and rested, gazing out across a landscape decorated with millstones, burning cities, and earthquakes. Meanwhile, the whole company of his employees departed for their annual picnic.

An errand-boy's shrill whistle pierced the dawn, rousing Christmas from the doldrums. He threw back the heavy blanket of gloom, and rose from his bed of confusion. Then, stripping off his grimy smock, he donned some other person's cast-off garments and limped towards the Factory gate, wearing a boot and a shoe.

The Factory breathed its contented holiday calm behind him. He schemed feverishly. With all the workers away, he could conveniently secure the gate against their return. Let them revel for the nonce in their mindless burlesques; they would arrive back to desperate unemployment and the whine of famished children.

But how to achieve the lock-out? He found his answer in the Gate itself, for there in the keyhole was a silver key. He rapidly spun the key in the lock, eyeing the suspicious shadows, and not pausing to query the key's presence. As he withdrew it his nostril twitched to a hint of musky odour.

He was in danger of going astray in the avenues of the wind, but that lingering token of his inamorata floated to his rescue. Though his senses were numbed by his mania, he was able to follow the twining thread of perfume that still whispered 'Bella! Bella!' to his brain.

# INTO THE NORTH AND INTO THE NIGHT

BELLA HERSELF had regained the Palace at last. Preparations for her departure took several days, but all the time gratitude to the red invader of her desolation glowed in her. She measured and stitched numerous changes of furry clothing for the journey, and lovingly marked her route upon an antique map. The way was open and inviting to that cold, passionless territory of her girlish dreams.

She hurried to the inner Room and, ignoring its plaintive appurtenances, stepped daintily over the fender into the hearth and commenced her bold ascent of the Chimney.

The route by which her Rubicotta had entered this alien Southern world would be for her the avenue of escape to the black and snowy night of the North. Already, as she rounded the Chimney's lower bends, diamonds of snow were glinting in the continuous rain of defiling soot.

The sound of Bella's last footfall in the Palace was echoed immediately by the urgent step of Christmas's return. Her perfume, a wilful emanation, led the slack-mouthed, panting seeker to those parts of the Palace where Bella's discarded toys still lay in forlorn yet faintly minatory attitudes of disuse, littering every room and passage.

What Christmas should have discerned, but could not for his vehemence, was that this mass of toys was exactly identical with the hoard in his sack. Every single piece had its twin – as Bella had hers. With the strange innocence of dementia, he heaped gross armfuls of Bella's juvenilia into his insatiable hold-all.

It was a disastrous action, only to be perpetrated by one ignorant of the basic incompatibility of precise facsimiles. Here was the green light the war-mongering golliwogs had been waiting for. The bag heaved and bulged, bidding fair to burst at the seams, and only exceptional footwork enabled Christmas to maintain his balance.

He careered through the Palace's torrid zones – the Hall of Mirrors, the Aquarium, the Dry Laundry, the Temple of the Fire God, the Casino, the Maritime Museum – reeling at last into that inner sanctum wherein the cheery flame of desire had once been kindled.

Now his acrobatic skills forsook him. With drunkard lurchings he went crazily and sweatily about, careering off the walls and upending the many chairs and birdcages. Hypnagogic illusions assailed eye and ear. The sun, framed in the Window – did it shine at noon or at midnight? The wind that belaboured the Room – did it drive snowstorm or sandstorm? The fire crackled in the hearth, and lured Christmas towards the Chimney by inexorable degrees.

Sibilant showers of soot and embers betokened the scrabblings of a hidden climber high above. It must be she! He sprang impulsively into the black rain and groped for handhold. Yet, try as he would, he could not insinuate his encumbered person into the gap. His overloaded, perversely animated sack was too bulky by far, but he could not let go of it. With insane lungings he pushed and squirmed until, with an obscene thunder, the sack exploded, strewing its contents over Room and hearth.

Thigh-deep in this festive morass, Christmas screamed imprecations at the cobwebbed ceiling till whitewash and plaster descended snowlike upon his piteous head.

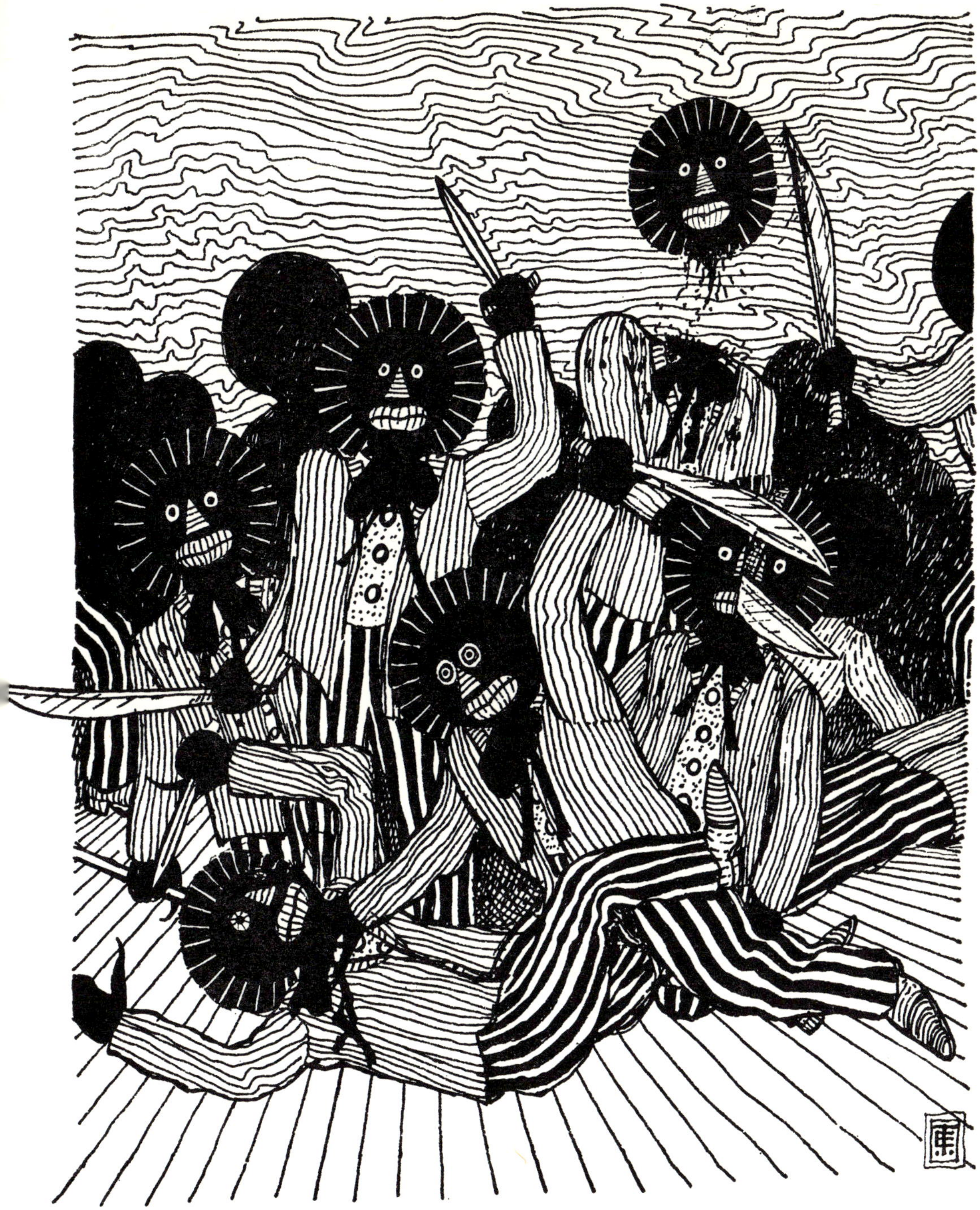

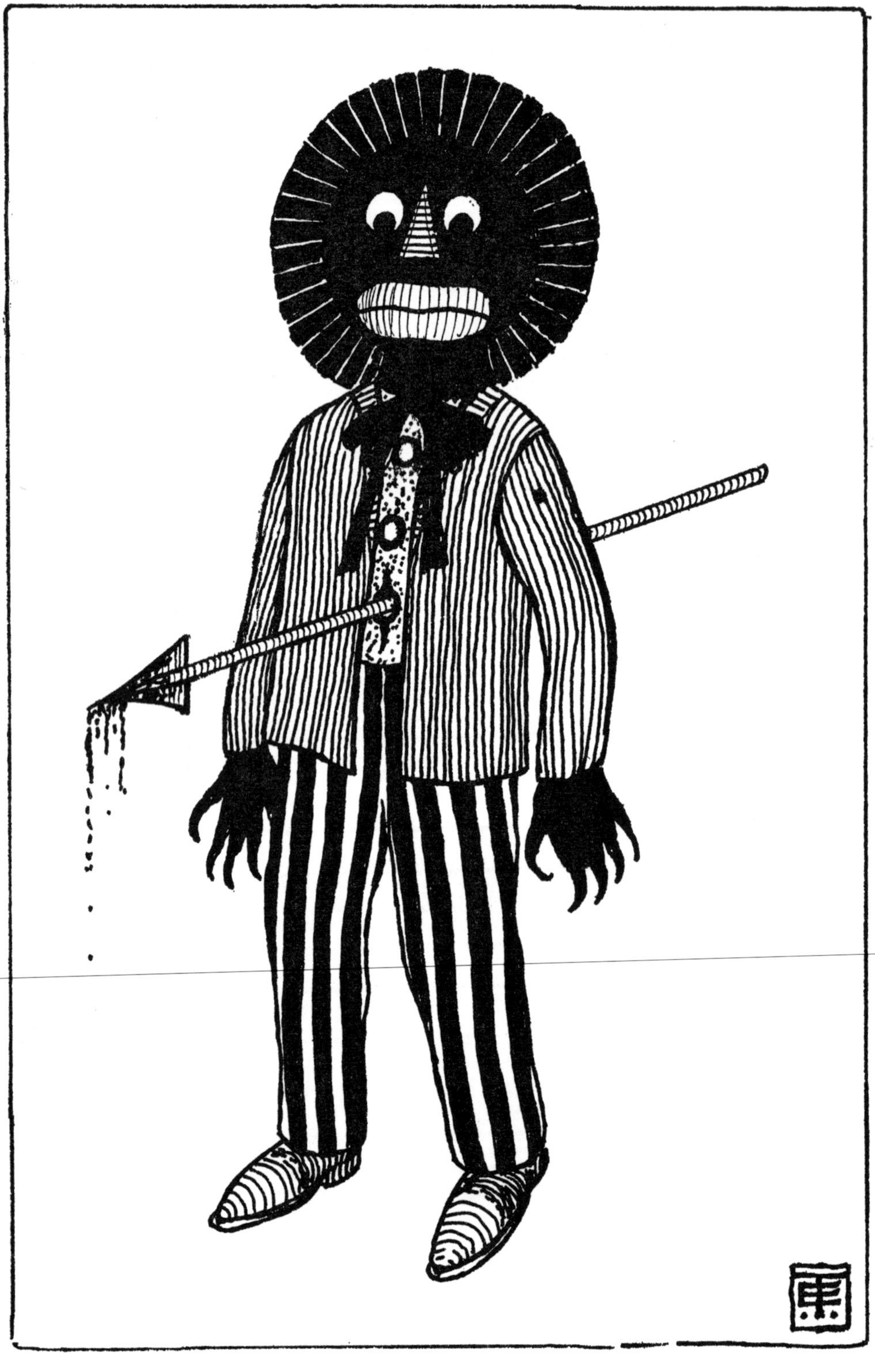

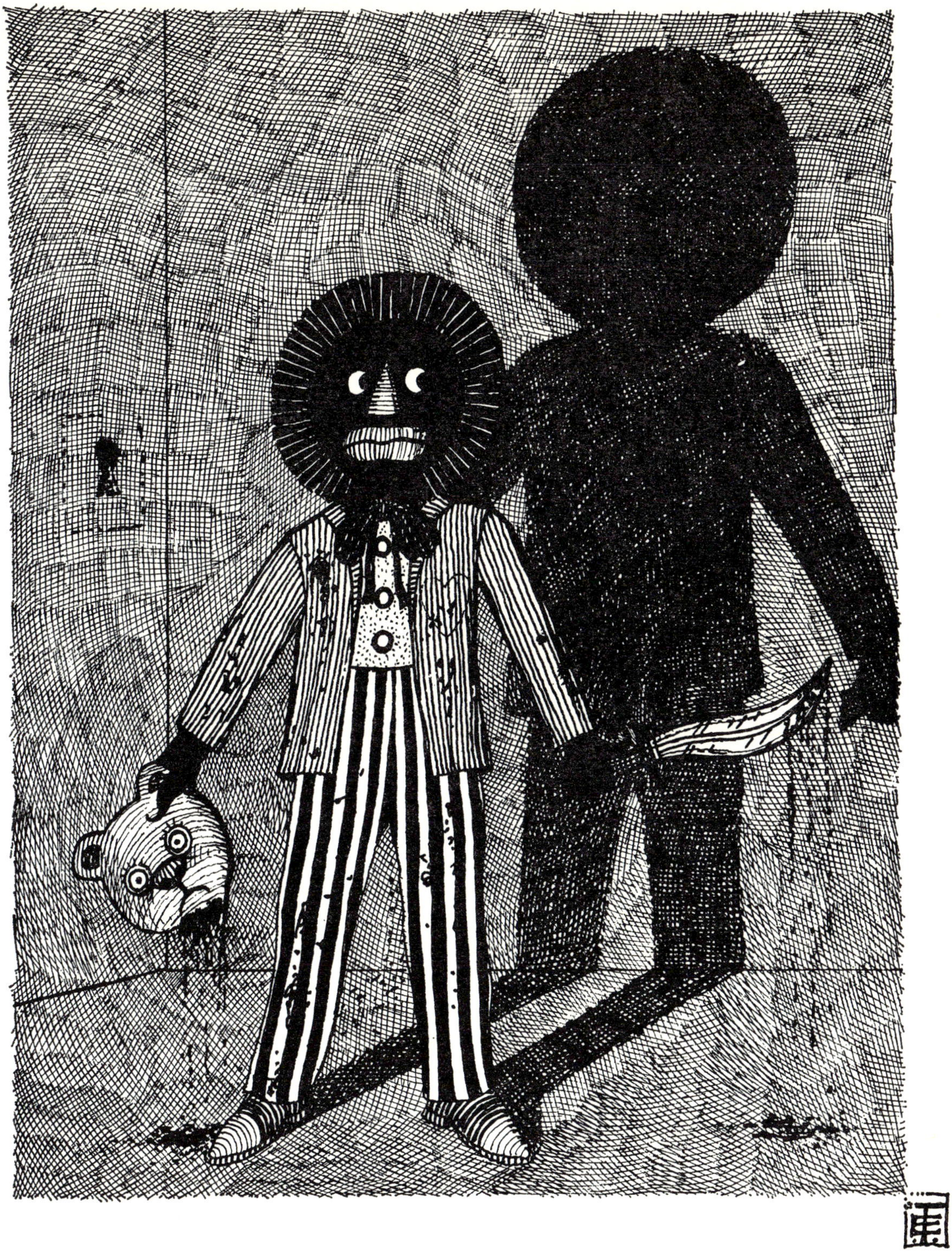

# TEN QUESTIONS FOR THE MUSROID READER

1 The Room in which Christmas now stands, is it:
   (a) His own original Room?
   (b) The Room that Bella built?
   (c) The Swiss Birthday Box?
   (d) The Cabin of a pirate brigantine?

2 Is the Factory:
   (a) In Intersol?
   (b) In Greenland?
   (c) In the Nameless Town?
   (d) Still in Christmas's pocket?

3 What is Bella's Destination? Is it:
   (a) Christmas's Room (Remnant of the Town)?
   (b) The Town itself?
   (c) Garibaldi's Tomb?

4 Where is the Musroid World? Is it:
   (a) In Christmas's sack?
   (b) In the Factory?
   (c) At the top of the Chimney?
   (d) At the bottom of the Chimney?

5 Are Intersol and Greenland:
   (a) The same place?
   (b) Two identical boxes?
   (c) Day and Night?
   (d) The picture and its frame?

6 Is the Nameless Town in the Room? Or is the Room in the Nameless Town? Perhaps both are in the Bran-tub?

7   Does the Chimney belong to:
    (a) Christmas?
    (b) Bella?
    (c) The Wolves?
    (d) The Smoke?
    (e) All of us?

8   What became of the Street?

9   Is the Chimney:
    (a) Part of the Factory?
    (b) Christmas's Clay Pipe?
    (c) A Street?
    (d) God's Little Finger?
    (e) Bella's Secret Treasure?

10  Do you keep your Factory Key on a silver chain?

## MADNESS

⁋ Handcuffed to his toys, Christmas was hauled to the cells of derangement.
⁋ He stepped through an unhinged door on to the crazy pavement of Sheba's Garden.
⁋ On the yonder side of the Street loomed the gigantic City of Nightmare. It reduced Christmas to the size of an unimportant somnabulist.
⁋ His storm-lantern signalled S.O.S. to a throng of preoccupied window-shoppers.
⁋ He followed the unpredictable track of the fly.
⁋ His terrors matched the hues of the rainbow.
⁋ Terror of blood.
⁋ Terror of sunset.
⁋ Terror of lions.

⁋ Terror of ferns.
⁋ Terror of forget-me-nots.
⁋ Terror of Midnight Savages.
⁋ Terror of Kings and Prelates.
⁋ Kicking the tin-can of infantile hopes down the alleys of wisdom, he woke the echoes of our earliest warfare.
⁋ Shamerack, bonemusic, earthwail, in waste moonlight, the white apocalypse of the staving chain.

## A WARNING TO ALL SLEEPERS

The Children of the Musroid World are asking the wrong questions.
   Why is Christmas snow whiter than the snow of Hallowe'en?
   Why do Christmas Trees harbour no birds' nests?
   How does Father Christmas get into our chimneys without disturbing the storks?

Such problems could safely be left to the horologists and chronographers, who have all the time in the world.

As it is, the most poignant questions remain unposed, and therefore unanswered. It never seems to occur to these poor little wretches that their touching requests, dispatched to Father Christmas year after year, are as futile as the prayers of atheists. Misled by charlatanic dreams, they acquiesce in delusion. The gifts they plead for are never the ones they receive, and the joys of their Christmas mornings are always ephemeral. They paint their mental portrait of a benign visitant who has all their dearest interests at heart. They wistfully suspend optimistic stockings from the rails of their shiny brass beds. It is time they were given the facts.

To begin with, all those letters addressed so carefully to the icy North never reach Father Christmas at all. They are opened by a cruel, smooth-skinned woman who cackles contempt at such ill-spelt lists and stuffs the rumpled leaves into her bosom. They lie there, forgotten for ever.

As for the toys which arrive each winter, neither correspondence or solicitude has anything to do with their bestowal. Father Christmas hardly ever thinks of children at all, and when he does his thoughts are exceptionally caustic. Most of the time, he is lusting after that worthless goddess who roosts, like a broody stork, at the top of his Chimney. She is the one toy he really and truly wants; every other toy, no matter how charming, is only a counterfeit Bella.

Yet, the old fool has a miser's brain, a jackdaw's eye, and a monkey's paw. If he jettisoned all his toys, he could speed up the Chimney to Bella as quick as a sailor's wink. But no . . . he sits there in steamy Intersol, tussling with a double greed, and sorting out the few toys he can torture himself into despising. This process takes roughly one year. Then, off he goes round the world at top speed, making dustbins of our cosy little musroid homes . . . And all this for the sole purpose of reducing the bulk of his sack.

Our innocents are being fobbed off with junk.

There is no telling how long this will go on, for there is a further complicating element. Having dumped his rejections, Christmas flies back to Intersol for another essay at attaining the *ne plus ultra* of ambition. But, during the interim, the tireless Factory has been working all round the clock, every day of the year, making toys of increasingly irresistible allure. Bella did not produce all those keys without foresight, and we should know the workers well enough to realize that they will seize any chance of spiting their betters.

Thus, the situation never gets any better. The miser gloats, the jackdaw blinks, the monkey snatches, and into the sack go further needless treasures. The scene is set for another busy New Year.

And still, with ingenuous laughter, we festoon our evergreens, slaughter our fowls, kindle our candles, and scribble our wishes. All is mummery? Christmas has no ear for our witless carols.

We remain without remedy for our festal afflictions. Christmas is still at it, and his self-multiplying stock is unlikely ever to diminish. Rubicotta, the Garibaldi of our ill-fortune, will have to be kept out of our chimneys and our nurseries, but how? ... All the almanacs are blank, and the princes of Church and State doubtless have reasons for their silence.

And what of Bella, the sea-anemone's mother-of-pearl dream?

Greenland is hers now, though it is Greenland no longer, and owns a new name and a new regime. Smoke and soot drift down in richer profusion, glaciers creak, icicles drip, winds and wolves howl in barren defiles.

Does she spare a thought for her Rubicotta, wreaking dark providence upon a bemused world, and all for her sake? Is she grateful still to the rebel who opened to her the sombre joys of paucity and, without knowing it, installed her as Queen of Wintersol, Land of the Frozen Sun?

Perhaps she does. Perhaps she is.

At all events, it is Wintersol that conceals the amethyst of our sobriety, Wintersol that frames the portrait of our doom, Wintersol that preserves the poisoned victuals of our ultimate meal.

Wintersol is the Magnetic Pole that woos our compasses, needling us with false portents of a Christmas that can never be.

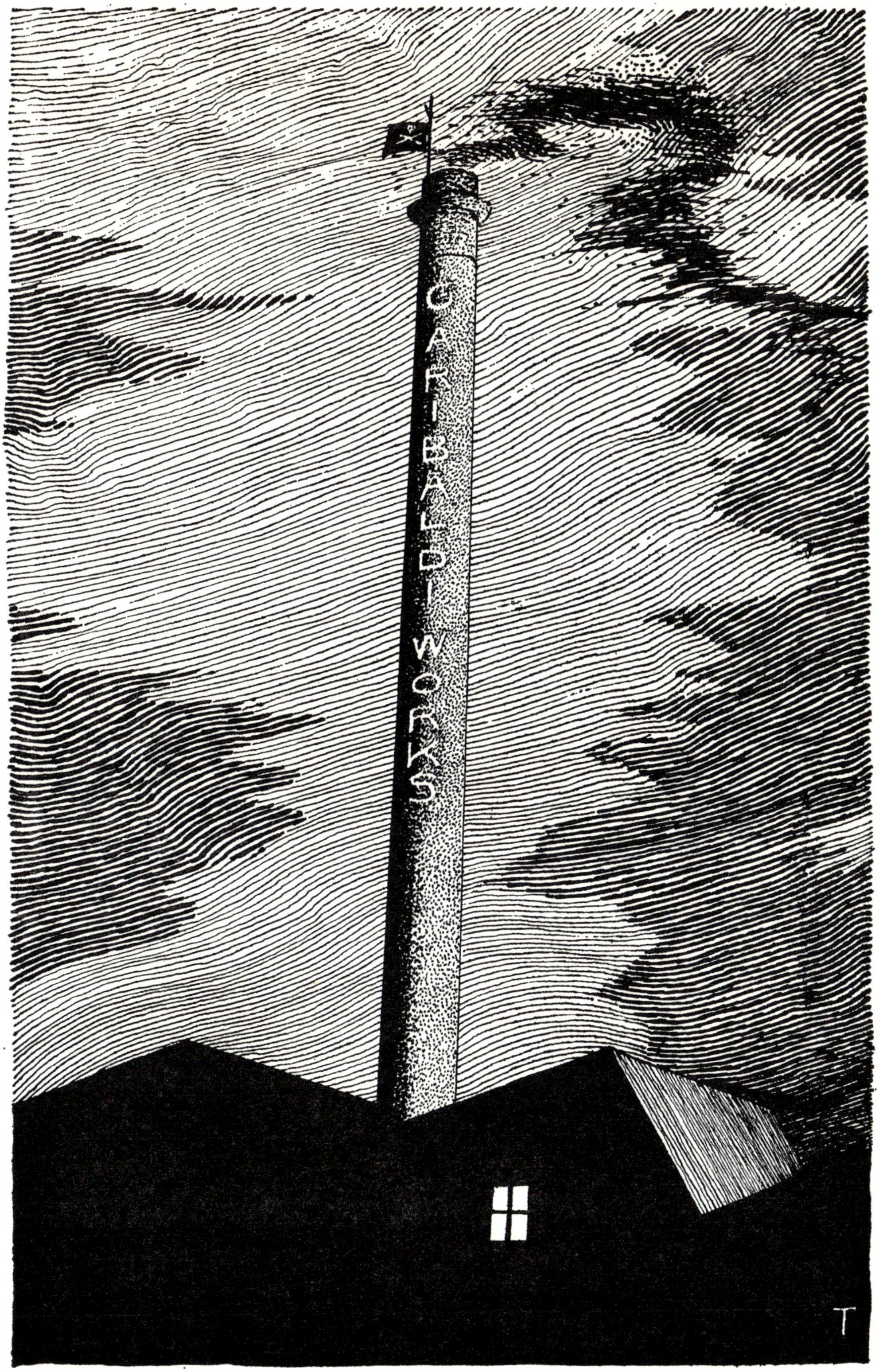
GARIBALDI WORKS
T